THE RED GREEN BOOK

QUANDO OMNI CHAPTER 11 FLUNKUS MORITATI

INTERNATIONAL POSSUM BROTHERHOOD

POSSUM LODGE

THE

RED GREEN BOOK

WIT AND WISDOM OF POSSUM LODGE

PLUS 100 PAGES OF FILLER

STEVE SMITH &

RICK GREEN

Prima Publishing

PRIMA PUBLISHING and colophon are registered trademarks of Prima Communications, Inc.

Library of Congress Cataloging-in-Publication Data on file
ISBN 0-7615-1235-7

97 98 99 00 01 AA 10 9 8 7 6 5 4 3 2 1
Printed in the United States of America

Cover and text design by Stray Toaster
Cover and inside photos by Today's Faces

PUBLISHER'S NOTICE: Every effort has been made to ensure that *The Red Green Book* meets the highest Possum Lodge manufacturing standards.

HAROLD HAS CHECKED THIS BOOK AND HE SAYS IT'S OKYA.

How to Order

Single copies may be ordered from Prima Publishing, P.O. Box 1260BK, Rocklin, CA 95677; telephone (916) 632-4400. Quantity discounts are also available. On your letterhead, include information concerning the intended use of the books and the number of books you wish to purchase.

Visit us online at www.primapublishing.com

This book is dedicated to anybody who fixes things by kicking them. With the exception of pets.

–Red Green

To Morag, Max and Dave. And to the courage, vision and spirit of the late Jerry Trainor, my mother Mary Muncey, and the members of Possum Lodge.

–Steve Smith

Dedicated to Gunda for everything. And to my father. He would have loved this.

–Rick Green

I wanna talk to all you middle-aged guys about how you feel tired all the time. I know what you're goin' through. Many's the time I'd be sitting in my living room listening to my wife and suddenly, just like that, my leg'll fall asleep. Or I get halfway up a flight of stairs and have to pull over into the slow lane to let the dog pass. And he's seventeen, which in dog years means he's... Old Man Sedgwick. As the years pile up you have less energy.

Now some doctors'll tell you it's the hours you keep, or what you eat and how much, or that you never exercise so you're seventy-five pounds heavier than you were when you last did anything. Actually, it's all in your mind. You see, your mind has quietly watched for forty years while your body flew over the handlebars on your bike or found the fast way down from a roof or went snap while lifting too much wallboard. Your mind is fed up with registering all that pain. So one day, when you're not using your brain—say when you're watching reruns of "Matlock," your mind sends out secret messages to your muscles ordering them to fall asleep or cramp up.

That exhaustion is simply self-preservation. So be thankful that your body is too tired to do the things you want to do. That tiredness is saving your life. Remember, I'm pulling for ya cause we're all in this together.

TABLE OF CONTENTS/
CONTENTS OF TABLE

This is the Contents of the Table that I sat at when I wrote this book.

HAROLD SPEAKS.

Okay. Three words. Three simple words that could change your life. Why gym class? WHY? What is the point? I mean other than to give people an opportunity to flick your naked flesh with towels, an opportunity that they wouldn't get in history or math. Who needs gym? What does this prepare you for? You show me a Chief Executive Officer who got to the top because he was good at dodge ball. Really? Like, I'm sure.

Where would we be if Henry Ford had become a field hockey player and then gone into coaching and then broadcasting?

Sure, there's a lot of great Russian gymnasts, but have you ever driven a Lada?

So I think I should be excused for the rest of the term. Especially before we have the dancing with the girls next week.

Think about it.

FOREWORD

Quando Omni Flunkus Moritati

(Count 'em)

BUYING TIP$

TIP$ ON BUYING A BOAT

Thinking of buying a new boat? Or an old boat? Or a yacht? Here are some things to look for and some things to watch out for when you're buying a boat.

GOOD IGN

+ Boat is in water and bilge pumps are not wailing at full speed.

+ Fire extinguisher hasn't been used up.

+ Ship is not named *Titanic 2*.

+ You don't have to take a submarine ride to view it.

BAD IGN

- Lifejackets strapped to outside of hull to "help it float."

- 460-horsepower outboard engine that you have to pull start.

- Transom held on with duct tape.

- Owner says, "She floats better in salt water."

- Teak hull has turned black with mould.

- Biggest safety feature is the word "HELP" painted on bottom of the hull.

- Bullet holes across the cabin.

INTRODUCTION

Well by golly here it is, my first book. And also the first book I've written. Finally my Grade 5 English teacher can be proud of me because this book is made up almost entirely of Grade 5 English. So for any of you young people out there who are not doing well in school or are having problems with your parents or have been stealing cars or blowing up buildings or whatever, the message is you can be your own person and eventually get to write your own book as long as you have your own television show and are willing to work for free. Which proves that the important part of growing up is communication.

I remember the long hours I spent talking to my mom or dad as some of my happiest memories. Whether it was convincing them that I didn't have any homework or asking them not to answer the door until the police car pulled away, it was quality time. Communication is the key to a successful life. That's why I like this book. I get to say whatever I want and you don't get to talk at all, which is my favourite type of communication. So I hope you enjoy it and I hope you appreciate the weekend I gave up to write it.

Red Green

P.S. If this book gets made into a movie, I'd like my part to be played by the accomplished actor and American president, Bill Clinton.

THE POSSUM PLEDGE

Upon becoming a member of Possum Lodge a member is required to place his or her hand over his or her heart, salute the flag, and solemnly repeat the Possum Pledge aloud while other members tease, razz, and throw stuff at them.

"I promise to try not to embarrass the fairly good name of the Possum Brotherhood or get caught doing anything that might get us into legal trouble or have us shut down by the authorities. I will lend a hand or a buck whenever I can, unless there's a really good reason. And on my honour, I won't swipe stuff that belongs to anyone more senior to me."

CHARTER

Ipso Facto

WHEREAS the Members of the International Possum Brotherhood agree to uphold the precepts and concepts and each other as the need arises, to build stuff and wreck stuff and generally alter the environment and quality of life for as many people as possible in a positive or negative way;

AND WHEREAS the Members accept that, from time to time, they will be called upon to provide resources for the benefit of the Lodge and its members. The use of these resources is subject to the wishes of the Lodge Leader or his designate, should he be unconscious or under arrest;

AND WHEREAS there will be a General Meeting in the basement of Possum Lodge on the third Saturday of each month, provided that the building is standing, and the basement is free of flood water, and the Lodge Leader's wife has not made other plans;

AND WHEREAS each Member has the right to bring up points of business or proposed projects or a short burst of self-indulgent whining, provided the Member has paid annual dues in full and in advance and has brought refreshments for all, liquid or otherwise;

AND WHEREAS each Member will try and build something neat out of stuff at least once a week;

AND WHEREAS all Members solemnly swear to share equally the responsibilities and rights inherent in Lodge membership, executing all duties and fulfilling all required obligations, and rewinding all tapes;

AND WHEREAS each Member's ranking in the Possum hierarchy will be based solely upon the duration of their membership in the Lodge as indicated by their membership number, this ranking will be the sole measure determining a member's standing in terms of dispensing or receiving wedgies from other members. No member shall wedgie a more senior member under threat of double wedgie. Wedgies will be administered in a manner befitting a member of the Brotherhood;

IT IS HEREBY RESOLVED THAT all Members agree to try to have a little fun in their lives and not take too seriously the things that can't be changed.

POSSUM LODGE RULES

RULE ONE: Firearms, explosives and nuclear devices are outdoor toys.

RULE TWO: Never buy anything that's too big to bury.

RULE THREE: It's easier to beg forgiveness than to seek permission.

RULE FOUR: Share and share alike, but not my stuff.

RULE FIVE: No scaling fish in the sleeping area.

RULE SIX: No talking during grace, prayers or playoffs.

RULE SEVEN: Don't solicit new members. We're losing enough money already.

If you'd like to join the Brotherhood, write to:

POSSUM LODGE

P.O. Box 3898 Station C
Hamilton, Ontario
Canada
L8H 7P2

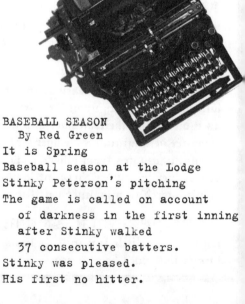

```
BASEBALL SEASON
   By Red Green
It is Spring
Baseball season at the Lodge
Stinky Peterson's pitching
The game is called on account
   of darkness in the first inning
   after Stinky walked
   37 consecutive batters.
Stinky was pleased.
His first no hitter.
```

✳ POSSUM LODGE EXECUTIVE ✳

> ✳LEADER/HEAD POSSUM✳
> Red Green

> ✳VICE PRESIDENT IN
> CHARGE OF SAFETY✳ Bill

> ✳SECRETARY/TREASURER✳
> Vacant

> ✳PAGE✳
> Harold

✳MEMBERSHIP AT LARGE✳ Couple of Guys

✳MEMBERSHIP AT EXTRA-LARGE✳ Almost Everybody

Facts and Figures on the
International Possum Brotherhood

The International Possum Brotherhood was founded in 1929 and was inspired by that year's performance of the stock market.

The purpose of this mutually exclusive organization was to bring together people who liked to accomplish things and weren't afraid to question obstacles like building codes, government regulations, and gravity. Although predominantly made up of middle-aged men, the Lodge accepts memberships from all genders, all races, all religious and sexual orientations, and in fact anyone who has access to tools, materials, big trucks, explosives, medical supplies, legal services or cash.

The possum was chosen as the icon for the organization because of its abhorrence of violent and destructive confrontation. The clever possum solves its problems through a cunning ruse known as feigning death. The founding members of the Brotherhood pledged to avoid confrontation and seek compromise thus making the possum the ideal symbol, lying on its back with its legs in the air— the internationally accepted compromising position.

The word "Brotherhood" was chosen because nobody was absolutely sure how to spell "Association" until their first album came out in the mid 60s. The "International" was both a feeble gesture to encourage global unity and a veiled attempt to qualify for a subsidy from the World Bank. Solicitations to the United Nations are ongoing.

Okay, for all of you who've been inquiring about Red Green Possum Lodge T-Shirts and Hats there are quite a few left, but no, we will not be selling autographed live possums. I don't know who started that, but it's just a false rumour. So can you sickos stop ordering them, especially in different sizes, and could that lady from the animal rights group just back off, okay? It was a joke.

Chapter 1 of Possum Lodge ran into financial difficulties during the first meeting when organizers announced that it was an open bar. Thirty-seven minutes later they were bankrupt and Chapter 2 was formed. This became the standard practice for the Brotherhood as the first ten chapters followed suit. The current Lodge is Chapter 11 and it faces a similar fate on a day-to-day, week-to-week, open bar-to-open bar basis.

The motto "Quando Omni Flunkus Moritati" is a Latin slogan, created by one of the Lodge members after watching Spartacus nine times. Loose translation: "When all else fails, play dead."

The original Charter of The International Brotherhood of Possums, listing all of the rules, regulations, obligations and rights was drawn up by the founding members, signed by each, officially notarized, and then misplaced. This document was held in such high esteem by the Possums that they never made the effort to draw up a new version. Finally, in 1979 it was realized that having a written charter would be good for the Lodge, lead to fewer arguments over who's allowed to do what and when, and possibly allow us to qualify as a charitable organization.

BUDDY SYSTEM

All right, you were at a party last night with your wife or your girlfriend or your female companion. And today you're being informed that you didn't have as good a time as you recall. This is because your partner did not appreciate you ignoring her totally eh, or flirting with other women, or doing that party trick where you play "God Save The Queen" by making loud wet noises with parts of your body. It's surprising how some people fail to enjoy live entertainment, but the point is you're now in trouble and you need some way to patch up the situation. Whenever you can, blame the booze. Just tell her that you had been over-served eh, and you weren't acting like yourself. If you don't drink of course, that's unfortunate 'cause it forces you to lie. You'll have to blame it on being really upset about say, the death of a close friend. But just remember when she asks you "Who died?" you're going to be expected to come up with a name. Just saying "old what's-his-name" won't cut it. What I do is name a friend I don't mind never seeing again. Or you could take the strong route and just tell her that's the way you are at parties and that'll be the end of that. And the end of going to another party with her. Or anywhere with her. Or anywhere with anybody.

```
NEW BIRTH
   By Red Green
It is Spring
The dog had two
   puppies
The cat had five
   kittens
I had eleven zombies
And my wife had a bird
```

Never drink anything you can't spell.

TEEN TALK

You know a lot of people my age are not big on the rap music. They say it isn't music. It's not even poetry. It's a bunch of folks getting revenge on the English language by using it as a set of drums. And the Rappers have names like "Ice Bucket" or "Zapp Zipper."

But I like rap 'cause you don't need any talent. This is something I could do. I can point different combinations of my fingers at the camera and chant dirty limericks to a metronome. I can add some under-dressed groupies in the background who are feeling their bodies like they're checking for moles. Edit it so fast that small animals have seizures and call myself "Ice Green." Or "Master Red Def Jam." Or "X Q Z Me."

I could be huge. Not good, but huge.

"This Saturday the Possum Lake Nudist Club is holding its annual dinner/dance. Dress: Black tie only. Music by Buffy and the Skintones. Due to mishaps last year, we will not be having the limbo dance or serving fondue, and the barbecue grills will be at chest height."

```
earthquake

We had an earthquake late last night
Shook the Lodge, gave us all a fright
Hit about 9 on the Richter scale
And bounced out the contents of the minnow pail
We went out the front till the danger passed
Cause if the Lodge falls down, it'll fall down fast
But it wasn't an earthquake shakin the ground
It was a kid in a Chevette with the bass turned up
way beyond a sensible level
```

POSSUM LODGE MERIT BADGES

"BADGES? WE DON'T NEED NO STINKING BADGES!"

From the beginning The International Possum Brotherhood has encouraged members to earn merit badges. But almost nobody did because it required some effort.

For example, to get your Ham Radio badge you had to learn Morse Code, learn a lot of rules, build a ham radio, and then get asked all about ham radios by a tester. Where's the fun in that?

No wonder we have boxes and boxes full of merit badges, sitting there unpacked since the day they were made back in 1932.

I decided it was high time we made some new badges and new categories that members would find more enjoyable and relevant—like napping, arguing sports statistics or putting up with rotten children. But that idea was dumped when Harold pointed out that we'd have to spend money to get new badges made. Waste not, want not. So I've decided to keep the old categories, but I've eased the qualifications.

Harold claims that by lowering our standards to meet the members' abilities we have compromised the Possum Brotherhood, demeaned the value of the badges, and pandered to the lowest common denominator, which is good because it'll match our television show.

BADGE AND REQUIRED SKILLS

Art Appreciation

1. Phone up Art Wilson, the guy who runs the barbershop in town.
2. Tell him how much you appreciate him.
3. Ask him if his fridge is running.
4. Say, "Well, you'd better go chase it then."
5. Slam down the phone.
6. Be able to explain in your own words why nudity is "artistic."

Astronomer

1. Rent all the *Star Wars* movies.

2. Build a telescope by grinding your own lenses and constructing a telescope housing OR also rent *Battlestar Galactica*.

3. Name at least one of the 12 constellations.

4. Read up about our planet, our solar system, our galaxy and explain what a nova is OR eat a Milky Way bar while watching *Battlestar Galactica*.

5. Visit a planetarium during one of their Led Zeppelin laser light shows.

Athlete

1. Select three (3) professional sports that you find interesting.

2. Watch those three sports on TV.

3. Describe in detail who won, what the key plays were and what you would have done better if only you were the coach, starting pitcher or quarterback.

Bird Watcher

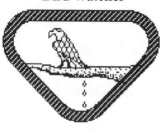

1. Watch some birds.

2. See what they do.

3. Try to figure out why they do it.

4. Try to guess what kind of birds they might be.

5. Ask your friend what he or she thinks.

6. Give 'em some stale bread. (The birds, not your friend.)

Book Lover

1. Buy a book. It must be a real thick book. Pamphlets, instruction booklets for power tools and greeting cards are not considered "books." Neither are comics, unless they are those *Classics Illustrated* ones.

2. Describe in detail as much of the plot, characters, setting and motivation as you can glean from reading the back cover.

Camper

1. Draw up a complete list of everything you'd take along on a two-week camping/canoe trip, draw up a complete menu for five campers and plan out the route your canoes would take. Spend at least five minutes on this.

2. Draw up a list of ten reasons why you can't go camping.

3. Go on a nature walk. ie. walk to the outhouse for the

call of nature.

4. Rent the movies *Meatballs and Meatballs 2.*

5. Barbecue some hamburgers.

Collector

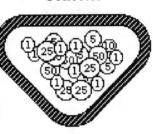

1. Make a collection from any of the following categories. Your collection must include at least 20 different items. You must be able to identify each one, and explain a bit about it to your tester.

Foreign coins	Foreign Stamps
Seeds	Beer bottle caps
Beer mats	Beer bottle labels
Beer bottles	Beer cases
Pill containers	Chewing gum
Balls of lint	Candy wrappers
Pizza boxes	Automobiles

Cooking

1. Read the ingredient labels on at least ten different kinds of junk food.

2. Make yourself a sandwich which includes at least ten (10) of the following ingredients:

White bread	Onion bun	
Ham	Yellow cheese	
Bologna	White cheese	
Pimento log	Orange cheese	
Mock turkey	Green cheese	Mock chicken
Spreadable cheese	Spam	Dill pickles
Mock Spam	Mayo	Butter
Margarine	Tomato	Lettuce
Salsa	Worcestershire sauce	Pickled Eggs
Peanut butter	Jam	Jelly
Honey	Nutella	Gravy
Cold Pizza	Salt	Sugar
Green pepper	Anchovies	Horse radish
Red radish	Those red things in the middle of olives	

3. Eat the entire sandwich (crusts incl.).

4. Keep it down for at least ten (10) minutes.

Crafts

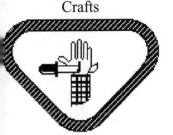

1. Make a unique craft out of macrame, beads, flowers or stale snack foods.

1. Describe what bugs you about people who ride bikes.

2. List three (3) examples of when some idiot on a bike almost made you crash into them.

3. Think of how we can get rid of these people on bikes.

Cyclist

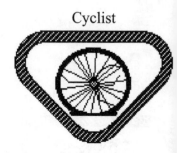

Dancer

1. Choose any style of dance music you prefer from one of the following categories:

WALTZ	MINUET
SAMBA	ROCK & ROLL
TANGO	COUNTRY & WESTERN
DISCO	BIG BAND
IRISH FOLK	BALLROOM

2. Play the music and do the following activities in time with the music.
A. Tap your foot.
B. Clap your hands.
C. Nod your head.

3. Discuss the artistic merits of lap dancers.

---

1. Watch a *National Geographic* special on PBS.

2. Research three (3) endangered species, and be able to describe why they are endangered, what can be done about it, and their value in the global ecosystem OR rent *Old Yeller* and the 4th *Star Trek* movie, the one where they come back to earth and save the whales.

Endangered Species

Explorer

1. Drive somewhere you never drove before.

2. Keep turning left and right until you're really lost.

3. Find your way home.

1. Drag your sprinkler out and set it up and turn it on.

2. Mow the lawn.

3. Spray your yard with weed killer, bug killer, and dog repellent.

4. Learn the names of five (5) flowers, their Latin names, the kind of conditions they thrive in, and then plant these flowers in an attractive grouping and water and fertilize them for one whole season OR buy one of those neat little cactus plants at the flower shop.

Gardener

Ham Radio

1. Own a radio.

2. Turn the radio up loud.

3. Sing along with a song on the radio and really act like a "ham."

---

1. Hire a really good housekeeper.

2. Draw up a complete list of housekeeping chores for the housekeeper.

3. Pay the housekeeper.

Housekeeper

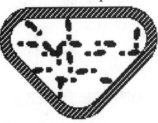

Interpreter

1. Rent three (3) foreign films without subtitles.

2. Try to figure out what they're saying.

3. Try to figure out what they're doing.

4. Try to figure out why they have no clothes on.

5. Learn at least ten (10) phrases or expressions in foreign languages such as:

   "Hasta la vista, baby!"
   "Ohh la la!"
   "Colonel Klink und Sergeant Schultz"

1. Make a large group of people laugh by telling a humorous anecdote, a sad incident from your childhood that you've never shared, or your secret ambition in life.

2. Have a personal habit or physical feature that people seem to find funny.

3. Rent all of the *Porkys* movies and critique them.

4. Learn four hundred (400) jokes, including at least two (2) that aren't dirty.

Jester

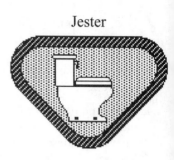

Musician

1. Learn to play any one of the following musical instruments:

SPOONS	TAMBOURINE
TRIANGLE	PITCH PIPE
CD PLAYER	AIR GUITAR
CELLO	

2. Drink a large glass of wine and then dip your finger in the last few drops and run it around the rim of the wine glass until it makes a high pitched note. Repeat with every size and shape of glass you can find until you fall down.

3. Learn to read sheet music. Not the notes, just the name of the song at the top.

4. Watch ten (10) music videos OR visit the Opryland USA theme park.

Native Lore

1. Rent *Dances With Wolves*.

Nutrition

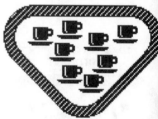

1. Have at least one (1) salad.

Observer

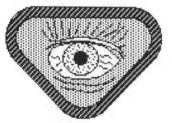

1. Develop your observational skills by watching at least three (3) of the following:

   a) animals in their natural habitats
   b) plant species from seedling to mature plant
   c) TV shows

2. Learn the names of at least five (5) of the following:

   a) wild flowers
   b) bird species
   c) members of your immediate family

3. Play "I-Spy With My Little Eye" with your tester until you win a game.

---

1. Get a pet.

Pet Keeper

2. Try to feed it every day.

3. If you forget and it dies, get another one.

4. Repeat steps 2 & 3 as many times as you can.

Heritage

1. Take an extra day off work to celebrate your provincial or state heritage.

2. Buy a big cake and have them decorate it with the name of your province or state and then eat it.

3. Make up a song in the shower about how great your province or state is.

4. Think of 10 things that stink about the other provinces or states and why yours is way better.

5. Show your support for your home by giving the finger to people with out-of-province or out-of-state licence plates.

6. Watch twenty five (25) sporting events on TV in which you cheer for a team from your province or state.

---

1. Rent *The Bells of St Mary's, The Ten Commandments* or *Nuns on the Run*.

Religion

2. Describe how the special effects were done in *The Ten Commandments* including the parting of the Red Sea and the stick turning into a snake.

3. Drive your family to church.

4. When you're sitting in your doctor's office, waiting for the results of an X-ray, promise you'll never sin again and you'll always go to church and you'll pray every day if God just gets you through this one thing. Repeat this every time you have a crisis in your life.

Scientist

1. Study motion by sitting in a rocking chair while you watch a sports event on your TV.

2. Study sound waves by playing with the volume on your TV set during a sports event.

3. Study light waves and electromagnetism by playing with the contrast, brightness and vertical hold while watching a sports event on TV.

4. Study infrared and ultrasonic waves by using your

remote to switch between two (2) or more sports events on TV.

5. Study the forces of gravity by pouring drinks and snacks during a sports event on TV.

6. Study chemical reactions by eating different kinds of food at the same time until you have to run to the washroom and you miss at least half of a sports event on TV.

Skier

1. Watch someone ski.

Skater

1. Watch someone skate.

Snowshoer

1. Watch someone snowshoe.

Swimmer

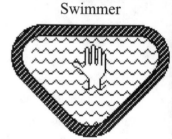

1. Watch someone swim.

Team Sports

1. Watch a team sport.

Tennis

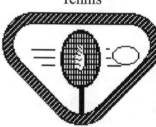

1. Watch a tennis game.

---

1. Find a way to get Pay-TV without having to pay for it.

2. Borrow money and don't pay it back.

3. Return all your empties.

4. Drive your car 'till it falls apart.

Thrift

And finally here are some badges that are really difficult to earn. Surprisingly, our lodge members have really started to chase after these badges. I think it just proves lodge members are not lazy.

Fishing

1. Go fishing every day for a year despite what your family or boss have to say.
2. Talk about fishing all the time.
3. Dream about fishing.
4. Read about fishing at your job.
5. Buy tons of fishing gear.
6. Go to every fishing show there is and be able to name every make, model, and manufacturer of every product.
7. Wake up one day and realize you've wasted a good chunk of your life, thrown it away forever on meaningless pursuits such as sleeping, eating and working. Vow to spend more time fishing.

Bowling

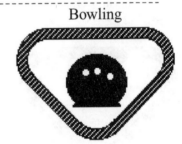

1. Go bowling every day for a year despite what your family or boss have to say.
2. Talk about bowling all the time.
3. Dream about bowling.
4. Read about bowling at your job.
5. Buy tons of bowling gear.
6. Be able to name every make, model and manufacturer of bowling products.
7. Wake up one day and realize you've wasted a good chunk of your life, thrown it away forever on meaningless pursuits such as sleeping, eating and working. Vow to spend more time bowling.

Boating

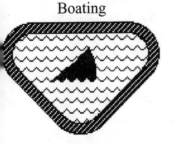

See Bowling OR Fishing

Hunting

See Bowling OR Fishing

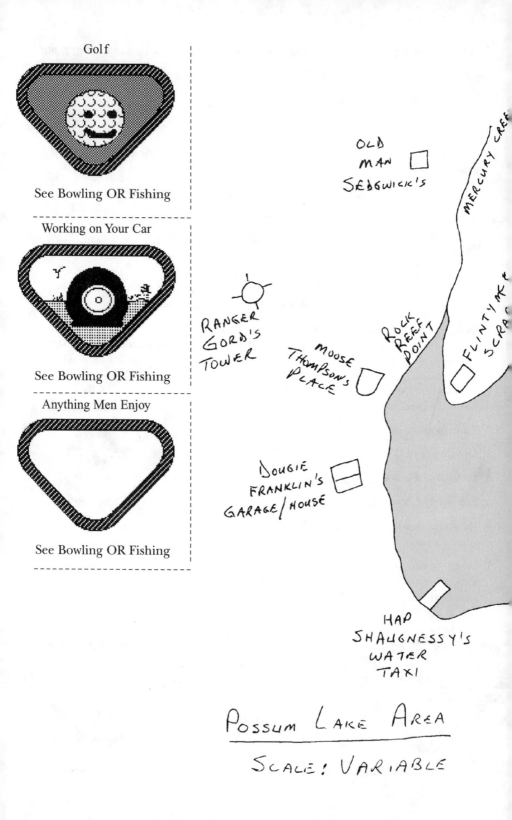

Golf

See Bowling OR Fishing

Working on Your Car

See Bowling OR Fishing

Anything Men Enjoy

See Bowling OR Fishing

OLD MAN SEDGWICK'S

MERCURY CREEK

RANGER GORD'S TOWER

MOOSE THOMPSON'S PLACE

ROCK REEF POINT

FLINTY MT & SCRAG

DOUGIE FRANKLIN'S GARAGE/HOUSE

HAP SHAUGNESSY'S WATER TAXI

POSSUM LAKE AREA

SCALE: VARIABLE

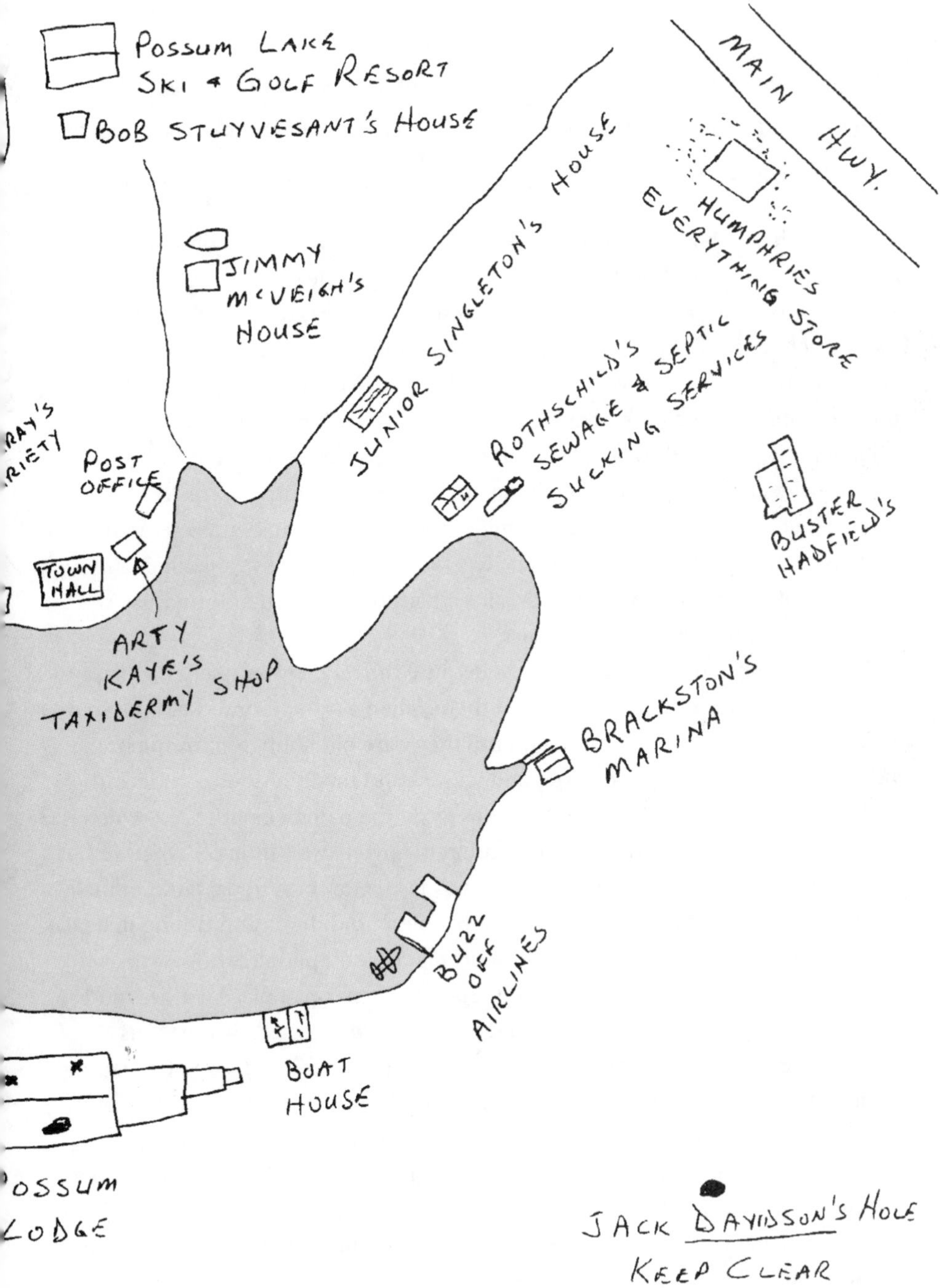

Possum Lake
Ski & Golf Resort

Bob Stuyvesant's House

Jimmy McVeigh's House

Junior Singleton's House

Main Hwy.

Humphries Everything Store

Rothschild's Sewage & Septic Sucking Services

Ray's Variety

Post Office

Town Hall

Arty Kaye's Taxidermy Shop

Buster Hadfield's

Brackston's Marina

Buzz Off Airlines

Boat House

Possum Lodge

Jack Davidson's Hole
Keep Clear

HISTORY OF POSSUM LAKE

Tracing the history of our area is a little difficult because there has never been a written record of anything that ever happened here. Mainly because nobody would be interested enough to read it. Except you. So here's the story as I know it:

In the middle 1800s a family of unemployed Vikings picked a beautiful unspoiled area in which to build their homes and start farming. Unfortunately they were unable to qualify for a mortgage and, as a result, were forced to settle at Possum Lake (which up until then had been a mosquito sanctuary). They more or less prospered for the next few years, although there were always rumours of inbreeding and other hobbies that people take up when they don't have cable TV.

Then in the early 1890s, Uncle Onan had an unfortunate accident while inventing the chainsaw automatic pilot, cutting down two-thirds of the local forest and one-half of his own legs. The logs generated from this incident were used in the construction of Possum Lodge. The legs were never used for anything, although there was talk of making them supports for a park bench but that would have required some imagination. And a park.

The Lodge was an immediate success because the men either needed a place to go or their wives needed a place to send them. Then a schoolhouse was built so that the kids would have somewhere to go until they were old enough to frequent the Lodge. Next came a dry goods store and a livery and finally a video arcade and movie rental. A town was formed and it was given the name Possum Lake which was also the name of the lake. This was confusing to anyone who thought about it, but certainly not the majority. The population was in the low hundreds, but eventually younger people moved in: a new breed of people who didn't mind fishing in a lake with no fish or hunting in a woods with nothing to hunt; people who saw the outdoors as a place to build things and then blow them up; a place for fires and inverted cars; a place where a man could try stuff he'd only seen in cartoons.

My dad brought me to Possum Lodge in the early fifties and I loved everything about it. The smells, the sights, the unreliability of everyone and everything. I joined the Lodge and started spending all my free time here, which is a big commitment when you have no job. After I married Bernice, I was elected leader of Possum Lodge and these remain the two biggest honours of my life. The day I get Bernice to actually come to a Lodge meeting will be the biggest day of my life and I'll probably keel over with unbelievable gas pains, but it'll be worth it.

I hope each of you is lucky enough to have a Bernice and a Possum Lodge in your life.

Okay, you got a problem in that your anniversary—which you seem to recall is coming up—is not coming up, it's gone by. It was yesterday and you pulled a complete blank. Total Anemia. So you need help digging your way out of this 'cause you are now in the deep stuff. Now you could just admit that you forgot about the anniversary and you feel real bad about it and it doesn't mean you don't care and would she please forgive you? But she won't. So instead, tell her that you had to postpone the anniversary because the special gift you got for her couldn't be delivered until the weekend. Which gives you 'til the weekend to buy something. If you then forget to go buy her the present, well, you're on your own.

Or, pull out your wallet and find last year's calendar on one of those little cards and point to it and say, "There's your problem, I had the right day, just the wrong year. I guess next year we'll have to celebrate our anniversary twice." That might work. If it doesn't you may not be celebrating it even once.

```
a guy who snores
This is the story of Lucy Dent
She had a husband who snored
And nothing would stop him and nothing would help
At least nothing that Lucy could afford
They always say you should wake a snorer up
So for years that's what Lucy did
The good news is it stopped the snoring
But Lucy now has 17 kids.
```

Home is where you hang your head.

I notice a lot of you teenagers are riding bicycles out there and I know it's good for the environment and everything, but what a pain. You drive in the middle of the lane and you come around corners just as if you were a vehicle or something. And you're practically invisible. What do you weigh, sixty pounds? And you got the spandex wrapping you so tight you look like a roll bar.

"For sale: Three speed bike, ready to run, or get it fixed and own a fifteen speed bike."

You're risking your lives out there. If we get into a misunderstanding as to who has the right of way, I'm in a van, you're in a helmet—you lose. I don't make judgments about how you young people wanna kill yourselves, but I think the bunch of you should either grow up and get a car or ride on the sidewalk. But not my sidewalk. That's where I park the van.

"For sale: used gas barbecue. Tank is rusted. Burners are rusted. Hoses are ruptured. Glass is cracked. Wheels are broken. 300 dollars or best offer."

"For sale, a big large brown and blue thing. I'm not sure what it is, but it looks real important and valuable. Contact Moose Thompson. 500 dollars or best offer. Will trade for a motor home."
Serious offers only there please...

This vehicle restricted to 55 mph –due to rust.

POSSUM LODGE IN 2095 A.D.

What will lodge life be like in 100 years? Here are our predictions:

Everyone will drive disposable paper towels. They will be powered by nuclear fusion and go from 0 to the speed of light in under 9 seconds. Naturally guys will try tinkering with their fusion reactors to get a little extra acceleration out of them.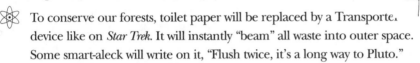

To conserve our forests, toilet paper will be replaced by a Transporter device like on *Star Trek*. It will instantly "beam" all waste into outer space. Some smart-aleck will write on it, "Flush twice, it's a long way to Pluto."

Boats will use anti-gravity pods to hover a few centimetres above the water surface. (So there won't be an annoying boat wake, and the hull won't be melted by the toxic chemicals in Possum Lake.)

Today many kids wear their clothes backwards—in the future they will wear them right side forward, but walk around backwards. Yet another generation with no idea where it's going.

New kinds of plastics, metal alloys, graphite compounds, ceramic materials and paper products will mean everyone has to own 435 different kinds of blue boxes to sort their different kinds of garbage.

All jokes and all forms of comedy will be banned to prevent anyone from ever offending some special interest group.

You'll be able to eat anything you want and never get fat. This will take the fun out of eating.

Instead of spending money, shoppers will just grab what they want and a computer implanted in their ear will keep track of how much they owe. If they get too far in debt, their head will explode.

A steak will cost over $5 million Cdn. (Which will be equal to over $800 US.)

Humans will be genetically engineered to eliminate disease, aging, and flatulence. Minor surgery such as gall bladder removal and vasectomies will be done at drive-in clinics while you sit in your car. Anyone who goes bald will have realistic looking hair tattooed on their head. Our brains will be five times larger, creating giant headaches.

There will be five different sexes. They still won't understand each other. The big debate in parenting will be whether to keep the test tube at home or have it raised in a lab. Making love will be a game from Nintendo.

Everyone will switch back to Beta format.

BUYING TIP$

TIP$ ON BUYING A NEW CAR

Thinking of buying a new car? Or an old car? Or even a van?

Here are some things to look for, and some things to watch out for when shopping for a set of wheels.

GOOD IGN

+ Both bumpers still on the vehicle.

+ All four fenders the same colour.

+ You kick the tires and they stay on.

+ Car is not up on blocks.

+ Odometer is not surrounded with claw hammer marks.

+ It suits your lifestyle—no sense buying a sports car if you have nine kids and family responsibilities. Unless this car is your ticket away from those responsibilities.

+ Interior of car not patched with duct tape.

+ Rich old lady selling the car and has no idea what it's worth; asks you to pick a figure that "sounds fair to you."

"Would the owner of an 85 Le Sabre with a blue door, primer red truck, grey primer fender, missing rear left fender, white trunk, and rusted roof please buy a new car for Pete's sake."

BAD IGN

- Major dents in the roof.

- Seller has "misplaced" the ownership.

- Bullet hole in back and dozens of air fresheners in the trunk.

- Floor mats are included in the price, but the engine is extra.

- Owner says, "Maybe you'll have better luck with this thing."

- Car was made in a Balkan country.

- The owner says, "I'm selling it 'cause I could never master the stick shift, and I'm sick of replacing transmissions."

- Previous owner converted car from rear wheel to front wheel drive.

- The air bags have been used seven or eight times.

- To take it for a test drive you have to hire a tow truck.

- Previous owner added a roll bar.

"Car For Sale. 86 Plym Reli, Frnt Whl Drv, Fac Air, Cust Uphol, AM FM, Blo Heat, Mint Cond, Rad Tir. Cont. Stink Pete Aft 6"
I've seen that car. "Pee Cra"

HAROLD SPEAKS.

Okay. Your First Date. Okay unlike me, many of you have never been out on a real date with a girl. Okay, first of all, don't try to kiss her in her front hallway when you pick her up and her parents are there. Second, don't make fun of people who play lotteries until you've ascertained if her family does in fact play them, or, and this is so unlikely I never would have imagined, they make their living selling lottery tickets.

Next, make sure her foot is in the car when you slam the door. And if it isn't, don't keep pushing the door thinking it's a seatbelt or something.

When the bill comes and you don't have quite enough money to cover it, don't burst out crying. Say something casual, like, "maybe we won't have fries with that." Don't take her to a German art film. Don't read the subtitles all through the film until she screams at you to shut up.

And finally, if she doesn't want to kiss you goodnight, don't ask her why. Thank you.

```
high school prom

Rummaging through my closet last night
I found the jacket I wore to the Prom
It was always a source of embarrassment
Not just the jacket but having to go
    with my Mom
They couldn't find my diploma
I asked them to look again
Then the principal pointed out in an
    unnecessarily loud voice
That I had dropped out half way
    through Grade Ten.
```

HOW WE MEASURE WIND VELOCITY

One of the main topics of conversation at Possum Lodge is our wind. It's important to know how windy it is if you plan to fish, sail, hang-glide, or wear a toupee.

Meteorologists (who know nothing about Meteors, even though they were a darned decent car) measure wind speed using the Beaufort Wind Scale, invented by Admiral Beaufort in the 1800s (which is called the nineteenth century—go figure).

Beaufort based his scale on the amount of canvas that a full-rigged frigate could carry. At Possum Lodge we don't have a frigate—although members often say something similar. So we have invented the Possum Lodge Wind-o-meter Scale.

CODE #	WIND SPEED	DESCRIPTION
0	0-1	Calm. Too calm. People get edgy. Smoke from the BBQ rises straight up, attracting buzzards. You can smell yourself.
1	2-3	Light air. Leaves on trees don't move. Smoke from BBQ rises at slight angle. You can still smell yourself.
2	4-7	Light Breeze. Leaves on trees move. You can smell the guy next to you.
3	8-12	Gentle Breeze. Everyone can smell everyone. Oriental wind chimes get on your nerves.
4	13-18	Moderate Breeze. Nuns make flapping sound. Leaves fly all over your yard.
5	19-24	Fresh breeze. Leaves fly all over your neighbour's yard. He yells at you, but you claim you can't hear him over the wind chimes.
6	25-31	Strong breeze. Difficult to walk. Drunks are blown over. Smoke from BBQ blows horizontally, right into your eyes.

CODE #	WIND SPEED	DESCRIPTION
7	32-38	Moderate gale. Trees move moderately. Boring uncle asks, "Windy enough for you?" Cheeks flap when you yawn. Aluminum patio furniture on the move.
8	39-46	Fresh gale. Nuns blown over. Falling down drunks held upright. Clothes blow off clothesline. BBQ blown over—smoke from burning deck blows horizontally. Trees move rapidly.
9	47-54	Strong Gale. Trees move slowly—across your lawn. Boring uncle says, "Windy? This is nothing. When I was young..." Your favourite toque blows off.
10	55-63	Whole Gale. Your favourite shirt blows off. Neighbour's gas BBQ comes through your window. Your newly sodded lawn is now someone else's newly sodded lawn.
11	64-75	Storm. You regret not hiring a pro to build your chimney. Boring uncle claims, "I've seen worse!" and is carried off by wind. People in trailer parks appear on tonight's news. Your underwear blows off.
12	Over 75	Hurricane. Your underwear blows off while you're indoors. People from trailer parks fly past your house. Your nose hairs whistle even when you're not breathing. You can't close your eyes. Even if you wanted to.

EMPLOYMENT ADVICE:

How to get and keep that all important first job.

Assert yourself. Show confidence. Nobody wants to hire a wuss. Arrive late for the interview and try to look a little rough. Don't give the false impression that you'll be getting up early to groom yourself before coming to work. Once you're in the boss's office, show you're interested in the job by asking important questions. How much does it pay? When can you take holidays? Does anybody check on you when you phone in sick? Are there any better jobs available at other companies? How often can you get a raise? How much severance will you get when you're fired? How many relatives and friends are covered by the medical plan? Which office supplies is it okay to steal? What's in it for me?

If by some chance you are not hired for the job, start legal action. So far, incompetents are still a minority in this country and are therefore protected by the Human Rights Act. Another thing you have going for you is that you have no idea how to do the job and thereby qualify for a government-assisted training plan. However, if you are competent, knowledgeable and experienced, you're out of luck.

Once you've got the job, try to fit in and get along with your new co-workers. Remember, everybody enjoys it when you make a joke about the size of their stomach. Always bear in mind that you're the new person so don't tell everybody how to do their job until the second day, but don't be too laid back either. Get their respect by forming a union. If they already have a union, form another one, one with a militia. Sit at the end of the table in the cafeteria, open your lunch box and pull out a really expensive sandwich, like roast beef or shrimp, or anything on a kaiser. Be sociable. Ask your co-workers what they are eating. Ask to try some.

Show an interest in your co-workers on the job too. Question them about what they do, what it pays and how a person would go about getting their job, theoretically of course.

Be a team player—get on the winning team and let them carry you.

The hardest trick is to believe in yourself. You're no better and no worse than the people you're working with, and there's no reason for them to treat you any differently than they treat each other. Keep that in mind in everything you say and do, and they'll never know this is your first job. Especially if you're in your mid-forties.

> ## No one finds it funny when you pretend to be a doctor.

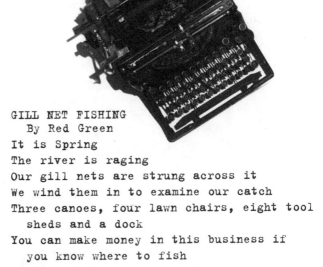

```
GILL NET FISHING
   By Red Green
It is Spring
The river is raging
Our gill nets are strung across it
We wind them in to examine our catch
Three canoes, four lawn chairs, eight tool
   sheds and a dock
You can make money in this business if
   you know where to fish
```

TEEN TALK

I want to talk to you teenagers about the way you dress. Let's make this clear—plaid shirts and baggy pants are not grunge wear, they're Lodge wear. We've been dressing like this since the invention of clothes and will continue to dress like this long after you've abandoned it for the next fashion fad.

And this brings me to my next point. You people are supposed to be rebelling against our generation, not copying us. Go get your own look—tinfoil clothing or chicken wire or latex paint or whatever. I mean it's embarrassing when a forty-year-old Lodge member is mistaken for a fifteen-year-old girl. Embarrassing. And dangerous. It's also a sad commentary on what today's fifteen-year-old girls look like.

So get out of the flannel and into sharp clothes now while you've got your youth and your looks. There's no point in dressing like a laundry hamper until you've got the face and body to go with it.

"Looking for shoes at a bargain price? Why not come by Stinky Peterson's Roadside Shoe Roundup. We have one of a kind shoes, all singles, all found along the side of the road. Lefts and rights, no pairs. Single Oxfords, single boots, even single big large furry slippers—which may actually be dead raccoons. I'm not sure."

God bless the entrepreneurial spirit of the small businessman.

"For sale, do-it-yourself mink coat, mink stole, mink jacket and mink hat. Kit includes one male mink, one female mink, a bag of mink food and a cage."

Some assembly required there obviously.....

HAROLD SPEAKS.

Okay. Finding a Summer Job. Okay guys at school ask me, how can I get a job like you have, Harold, producing and directing a small TV show as a stepping stone to a career in real television? And I say, work hard, learn all you can about the medium and then when you're ready, ask your uncle if he needs some cheap help.

But you also have to be concerned with your appearance and demeanour. To get hired anywhere, in computers, muffler replacement, whatever, you need to be able to present yourself in a presentable presentation. Get a resume. List all the things you've done. Cut out the illegal and dirty stuff and emphasize the positive. Like okay, say you were caught for shoplifting when you were nine, then say, "experience in retail." Or if you're still a virgin say, "willing to learn."

"Are you tired of being picked on by bullies?" You bet. "Why not learn the ancient Oriental art of self defence known as Su Shi. Learn to overcome attackers with raw fish and carving knives. Contact Junior Singleton." Wasn't he offering a cooking course last week?

The thing is to make the most of what you have. And that means hiding a lot of it. Thank you.

You can lead a horse to water, but you can't make a good living at it.

BUDDY SYSTEM

Okay so you're splattered across the couch, watching TV, grazing the dial with your thumb tapping the remote like you're sending Morse Code. Phase One: Your wife asks you to quit flickin' all over the place. It's going to give the dog a conniption fit. Just find something and stay with it. So you reply you can't decide what to watch until you find out what's on. And you say it all without taking your eyes off the set.

Phase Two: Your wife suggests you look in the TV guide which is what it's for, eh. Explain you left your reading glasses on the table. And the TV guide's on the back of the toilet.

Phase Three: Your wife picks up some knitting or a book. Finally you settle on what you want to watch— a comedy, a sports event and something with guns shooting—and you're keeping yourself apprised of what's going on on all three. Then something really good happens on the comedy, eh. Like Hawkeye is going to get a girl for Radar. So you settle on it for awhile. Your wife looks up. Then the commercials start and you're back on the road thumbin' your way to a better show.

Phase Four: Your wife gets up, exits the room, goes out and buys her own TV and files for divorce. It can happen. Life is about choices. So is television. You can't have a successful marriage and a TV remote. I say go for the successful marriage.

Unless the playoffs are on.

A dog is a man's best friend. Women know better.

MEET YOUR MEMBER.

Okay. Celebrity Profiles. Okay there is a magazine for teenagers which contains celebrity profiles, but they haven't gotten around to us yet because they have no idea who we are which delays things. Understandably. I have no problem with that. So rather than wait, I thought I would do a little celebrity profile on each of us. So folks it's time to "MEET YOUR MEMBER".

BILL SMITH

FULL NAME: William Deke Smith

AGE: 38

OCCUPATION: Each week Red joins me for an adventure which we call "Adventures With Bill." We have fun with kayaks, grappling hooks, golf clubs, etc. It's very educational—I've never made the same mistake twice. Or broken the same bone twice.

MARITAL STATUS: Married to a very nervous woman. Three very hyper kids.

HOBBIES: Amateur Chemist. Crash test dummy.

MAJOR TURN ONS: Pushing the envelope. Freefall. Ignoring the instructions that come with things.

MAJOR TURN OFFS: Gravity. Impact. Losing my handhold. Splints. Lawsuits.

FAVOURITE COLOUR: Anything but blood red.

FAVOURITE FOOD: Sugar and food colouring. (They really get me UP!)

FAVOURITE MOVIES: "The Stunt Man", "Patton", "Dumbo".

FAVOURITE BOOKS: "Learn First Aid"

PROUDEST ACCOMPLISHMENT: Doing all those "Adventures with Bill" and living to tell the tale. If you call this living.

LODGE RESPONSIBILITIES: Testing out stuff that might be dangerous.

WHAT TOOLS DO PROS HAVE IN THEIR TOOL KITS?

And what do I have in mine?

The home handyman usually has between 40 to 60 different tools in his tool box. Professional builders or carpenters carry between 275 and 300 different tools in their tool kit. I carry 5.

THE RED GREEN "VERY PORTABLE" TOOL KIT:

A hammer   A saw   A screwdriver   Pliers   Roll of duct tape

Those five tools have everything I need to fix a loose chair, rewire a socket, or add an addition to the house. Here's a list of all the tools you can buy if you're absolutely made of money, and beside each is the tool I use to do the same job.

WELL-STOCKED TOOL BOX	RED'S TOOL BOX
HAMMER	HAMMER
HAND SAW	HAND SAW
3 SCREW DRIVERS (SLOT HEAD)	SCREWDRIVER
3 PHILLIPS HEAD SCREWDRIVERS	HAMMER
3 ROBERTSON HEAD SCREWDRIVERS	HAMMER
3 CHISELS	SCREWDRIVER
CROWBAR	HAMMER
WRENCH	HAMMER
HACKSAW	HAND SAW or HAMMER
MITRE SAW	HAND SAW
SABRE SAW	HAND SAW
RECIPROCATING SAW	HAND SAW or HAMMER
METAL RULER	Metal edge of the HAND SAW blade
2 SLIP JOINT PLIERS	1 SLIP JOINT PLIERS
LINEMAN'S PLIERS	1 SLIP JOINT PLIERS
CHANNEL TYPE PLIERS, VICE GRIP PLIERS, END CUTTING NIPPERS, NEEDLE NOSE PLIERS, LONG NOSE PLIERS, PIPE WRENCH, ADJUSTABLE WRENCH, RATCHET WRENCH, OPEN END, BOX END WRENCH SET, ALLEN WRENCH SET	1 SLIP JOINT PLIERS
RUBBER MALLET	HAMMER
WOOD MALLET	HAMMER

WELL-STOCKED TOOL BOX	RED'S TOOL BOX
NAIL SET & NAIL PUNCH....................	HAMMER
ELECTRIC DRILL..........................	HAMMER
HOLE SAW	HAMMER
PLANE.................................	SCREWDRIVER
PUTTY KNIFE	SCREWDRIVER
SCRAPER...............................	SCREWDRIVER
SOLDERING IRON	DUCT TAPE
WOOD GLUE	DUCT TAPE
STAPLE GUN.............................	DUCT TAPE
COMPASS	Round roll of DUCT TAPE
ROUTER & ROUTER BITS..................	SCREWDRIVER
CARPENTER'S LEVEL	Eyeball
T SQUARE..............................	Eyeball
TAPE MEASURE	Eyeball
PROPANE TORCH, SOLDER	DUCT TAPE
PIPE CUTTER...........................	SAW
METAL SNIPS	SAW
"C" CLAMPS	HAROLD
VICE..................................	HAROLD
PIPE CLAMP	MOOSE THOMPSON
WIRE CUTTERS	PLIERS
WIRE STRIPPING TOOL	PLIERS
FUSE PULLER...........................	PLIERS
ELECTRICIAN'S PLIERS	PLIERS
CONNECTING NUTS.......................	DUCT TAPE
FUSES	pocketful of change
CIRCUIT TESTER........................	HAROLD'S FINGER
LATHE.................................	I don't build round things
POWER JOINTER	I don't joint things
POWER DRILL PRESS	HAMMER
GRINDER...............................	HAMMER
BELT SANDER...........................	HAMMER
PAD SANDER............................	HAMMER
VARIOUS FILES (Wood & Metal)	SCREWDRIVER
HOT GLUE GUN	DUCT TAPE
TOILET PLUNGER........................	HAROLD

I think you can see that my tool list proves a point I have always lived by—
imagination costs nothing.

HANDYMAN CORNER

DUMPSTER COTTAGE

Everybody likes to have some place they can go to get away from it all, or get away from the law or whatever. But not everyone can afford a cottage, so here's a handyman project that will fit inside almost any budget. I'm assuming you have a piece of land somewhere, but even if you don't, it's a big country and they're not going to check every square mile every year so you'll get at least one season out of wherever you build.

Step One: Call the biggest garbage collection agency in your region and ask them to drop off the biggest dumpster bin they have, and it must have a heavy lid. Tell them you'll be clearing a property and you'll have a lot of garbage for them to come and get when it's done. In most cases they will deliver the dumpster and leave it for no charge. Make sure they set it down between two big trees with high crotches. (High crotches are very important for almost everything you do outdoors.) See Diagram A:

Diagram A

Step Two: You will need two spare tires off a car or a small truck. If you don't have any sitting out on your porch, you can swipe them from the trunks of BMWs because people who drive those cars would never change their own tires anyway. Okay now you must remove the tires from the rims. Gas stations have special equipment for that, but you could try it with a crowbar and an oar. The easiest way is to just burn them off. Leave the area while they're burning. You should have no trouble finding your way back. Just follow your nose. Scrape the residue off the wheel rims and attach them to opposite sides of the dumpster as shown in Diagram B.

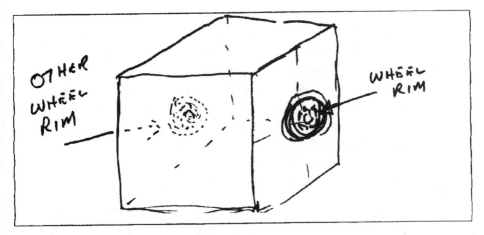

Diagram B

I recommend you weld them on or you could drill holes and bolt them or you may want to use the Handyman's Secret Weapon—duct tape. These rims have to support the entire weight of the dumpster so use lots of tape.

Step Three: Cut a door and a window in each side that has a rim. Again I recommend an acetylene torch, but you can use a tempered axe or even a chainsaw if you really like sparks. Once that's done, move your living room furniture into the dumpster, set it on the floor and bolt it into place. Lamps can be glued to tables. Wind your jumper cables around your appliances and hook them up to your car battery which will magnetize them. Then bring them into the dumpster and stick them on the wall as shown in Diagram C. Attach your bedroom furniture to the inside of the lid of the dumpster with self tapping screws. And the fourth wall can be done as a family room or den or whatever suits your particular lifestyle. Again all furnishings must be fastened securely to the wall.

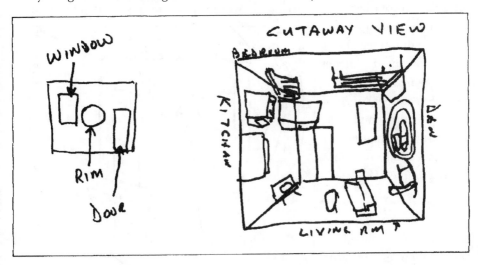

Diagram C

Step Four: To lift the dumpster up into the trees, you'll need a long chain or thick rope attached to the top of the dumpster. We tried it with a garden hose and I wouldn't recommend it. Rubber can really sting. Okay, so take the rope and swing it over something high and strong like an overhanging tree branch or railway bridge. Attach the other end of the rope to your van as in Diagram D. As you drive away, the rope will lift the dumpster up in the air. Unless the dumpster is heavier in which case it will lift the van in the air. To avoid this problem, invite your overweight relatives over and stuff them into the van. Drive forward slowly until the dumpster is in the air with the rims over the crotches. Back up until the rims drop into place, securing the dumpster.

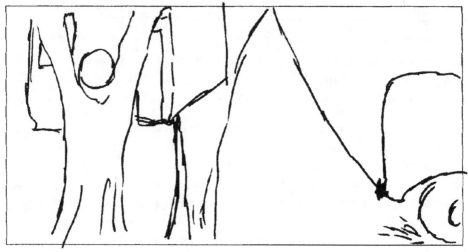

Diagram D

Step Five: Get in and enjoy your summer. Sit in the living room and amuse yourself with your favourite television shows. When you need something from the kitchen, just walk towards it and the dumpster will rotate, bringing the kitchen to you. Same thing when it's bedtime or you need some quiet time in the den. Just walk towards whichever room you want. It's that simple. (🌲)

(🌲) Not recommended for Dutch Elm trees or hillsides.

Diagram E

Okay, time now to meet the man who protects all of the Possum Lake area from fires, many of which have been started at his tower. He's been alone up there for a long, long, much too long, time yet he continues to be an inspiration to people who have to deal with loneliness, rejection and how to comb your hair after being hit by lightning.

RANGER GORD

FULL NAME: Gordon Tuzo Sisyphus Ranger. (Since my last name is Ranger, I prefer to be called Ranger Gord rather than Ranger Ranger.)

AGE: I'm not sure. What year is it?

OCCUPATION: I man Fire Watch Tower 13. Every day of the year for the past 15 or 16 years. I'm not sure exactly how long. What year is it again?

MARITAL STATUS: Very much single.

HOBBIES: Thinking about stuff. Trying to remember the faces of people I used to know. Whittling trees into toothpicks. Making a real live woman out of Fimo.

MAJOR TURN ONS: A visit from anyone or anything. Pen pals. Valerie Harper.

MAJOR TURN OFFS: Stray lightning. Bathing during black-fly season. Wondering what episodes of "Welcome Back Kotter" I've missed since I've been here.

FAVOURITE COLOUR: Forest green & Sky blue.

FAVOURITE FOOD: Birchbark. No really. It's great.

FAVOURITE MOVIES: "The Omega Man"

FAVOURITE BOOKS: "Waiting For Godot", "The Catcher in the Rye"

PROUDEST ACCOMPLISHMENT: I've never failed in my assigned duty to stand guard and keep watch for forest fires.

LODGE RESPONSIBILITIES: Watching for forest fires. Waiting and watching. And waiting. And waiting. And waiting.

BUYING TIP$

TIP$ ON BUYING A HOME

Thinking of buying a new home? Or an old home? Or a cottage? Here are some things to look for, and some things to watch out for when buying something that is going to put you in hock for the rest of your days.

GOOD IGN

+ The owners are still in the country and alive.
+ No large animal droppings in the attic.
+ Glass in all the windows.
+ It was not built on an ancient tribal burial ground where many graves were disturbed.
+ You're allowed to inspect all the rooms.
+ Nothing breaks off when you touch it.
+ More than fifty feet from all major airports, railways, dumpsites and active volcanoes.

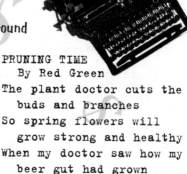

PRUNING TIME
By Red Green
The plant doctor cuts the
buds and branches
So spring flowers will
grow strong and healthy
When my doctor saw how my
beer gut had grown
He made me cut back a few
Buds myself

BAD IGN

- The word "!redruM" is carved in the walls.
- Their grandfather is included in the price.
- The real estate agent warns you not to walk in the middle of the floors where it's soft.
- The sellers are "very motivated" to sell because they fear for their children's safety.
- High-water marks on the basement walls.
- Turquoise kitchen appliances.
- Bullet holes in the bathroom.
- The real estate agent says you can't flush the toilet until after you've bought the place.
- The house has been treated for termites nine times in the last two years.

I want to talk to you guys who are just celebrating your fiftieth birthday, or are just recovering from the hangover. You'll know what I'm talking about when they bring you your birthday cake and tell you that each candle represents a decade.

When we reach mid-life most of us review our accomplishments and we take stock of our position in the community, and our careers, and our family situations and we conclude: life stinks and we really blew it. But I say, look on the bright side: everybody's life stinks. Nobody gets what they want. Millionaires wish they were billionaires. Married guys wish they were playboys, and playboys wish they could find someone worth marrying. Maybe you regret not marrying your first sweetheart when you were both sweet 16. Well don't forget, you're not sweet 16 and neither is she now. If you passed each other on the street today you'd both think "Boy some people really let themselves go."

So if you're feeling your life is over and you blew it, remember—it's only half over, and you only half blew it. And then get out there and finish the job. Remember, I'm pulling for ya 'cause we're all in this together.

```
THE MATING RITUAL
   By Red Green
It is Spring
As I look from my
   window
I see dogs mating on
   my front lawn
Cats mating on the
   shed roof
Moose rutting in the
   forest
I watch mildly
   bemused
Then I go to the
   workshop and design
   a new trailer
   hitch.
```

*If I had my life to live over,
I'd live it over a bait shop.*

HAROLD SPEAKS.

Okay. The Future of the World. Or specifically, how I hurt myself shaving. You know we have an educational system that can teach me the capital of Prince Edward Island is, uh Fredricton or no... it doesn't matter. They teach you all sorts of ivory tower stuff you'll never use, but they don't teach you about life. My parents talk about big issues, but who was there to warn me about electric shavers? Surely I wasn't the first person to get their nose hairs caught in an electric shaver? Surely I wasn't the first person to almost cut off their lip and have a shaver grinding its way up their nose into their brain.

I know you've all had this happen, but we're not going to see any changes until someone with a media profile like myself steps forward and makes it an issue. Why aren't there labels warning about nasal use? Nobody in the Emergency Ward could answer that one. Nuclear war is one thing, but this really hurts.

You can bet if I have a son, it'll be the first thing we talk about. Thank you.

Here's an open invitation from Ranger Gord, who, as I'm sure you know, has been manning the Fire Watch Tower on Possum Lake for the past 16 years. "I'm having a pajama party, bring all your old ABBA albums."

Okay, here's a personal ad "I am a single, white, male, with a great personality, dynamite looks, and a body that doesn't quit. Unless I tell it to. I like long romantic walks, and continental dining like canned spaghetti and French Crullers. I am looking for companionship, commitment or a date. Contact H. Box 0001." Boy, doesn't he sound like a catch for some lucky lady? It is lady. I know he didn't say women only, but I don't want guys calling. It's a straight guy. I'm sure.

MODERN MYTHS

Every civilization has had its myths and legends. The Greeks had "Herpes and the 7 Labours," the Romans had "Leda and the Big Bird," and the Europeans had Brother Grimm stories like "The Shepherd Boy Who Cried Woof!" These stories all had a moral. Today's youngsters are sadly lacking in morals.

Unfortunately young people today are not interested in legends and myths. Although they do seem to enjoy lying. But young people don't see any relevance to stories about gladiators, ancient warriors, flying gods, and golden-haired maidens, unless they're part of a Metallica video. Whereas in my day we had to learn all this mythology crap.

That's why I have updated some of the classic myths, fairy tales, fables, and legends to make them more relevant to today's youngsters.

STARSKY & ICARUS

Once upon a time there was a father-and-son team of private detectives named Starsky and Icarus. They drove a solid gold chariot with a 427 fully blown hemi engine, racing suspension and roll cage. Starsky and Icarus did battle against the mighty Zeus, the god of arms smugglers. Zeus was sorely angered. And he hurled lightning bolts and thunder, using state of the art special effects. But to no avail. Finally Zeus took one of his own ribs and turned it into a goddess no man could resist because she looked like Julia Roberts. The goddess lured Starsky and Icarus to a distant island which had a strip of seedy motels. Then she cast a spell over them and they fell asleep for a hundred days and a hundred nights. When Starsky and Icarus awoke, they were in a cave, and guarded by a twelve-headed lion known as the Committee-ausaurus Rex. The two could never escape because at least six of the heads were always awake. Finally

"427 hp Fully Blown Chariot."

Starsky removed a thorn from the paw of the monster, but only three of the heads were grateful. So Icarus started talking about which was the best rivalry in hockey—Toronto vs Montreal, or Calgary vs Edmonton, or the Rangers vs the Islanders. Soon the twelve heads were fighting amongst themselves, and the monster swallowed its own heads and its tails until nothing was left but a big set of lion lips. Then Starsky and Icarus found some hang gliders and tried to fly to safety. But despite his father's warnings, Icarus flew too close to the sun and was toasted by the ultraviolent rays.

MORAL OF THE STORY: Hang gliding is dangerous, so listen to your parents.

SNOW WHITE & CINDERELLA & RED RIDING HOOD & GOLDILOCKS

Once there were four princesses. Snow White had very, very white skin because she wore so much makeup. Cinderella was called Cinderella because she hated her own name, Debbie, due to a lot of hostile feelings towards her mother which she had not worked out. Red Riding Hood was named Red Riding Hood because her parents were from California, and named their kids stuff like Moon Zoom 3 and Dweebo. And Goldilocks was called Goldilocks as part of the witness protection program.

Anyway, these four girls had many romantic adventures and fell in love, and wore beautiful gowns, and never were sick, or had real problems, and they were always beautiful. And it became an Aaron Spelling production and made a fortune in reruns.

MORAL OF THE STORY: Defer on the licence fee and go for ownership of the series with distribution rights.

HANSEL AND GRETEL

Hansel and Gretel were a couple of wise-cracking New York singles who fell in love and had their own TV sitcom with some wacky friends. Then one day they got lost in the woods and came upon a house made of beer bottles. They didn't know the house belonged to an evil witch with a severe drinking problem. The witch's brew was a lager, on tap. Hansel and Gretel drank the witch's bubbly potion, and then some more, and some more. And then one for the road. By and by they were talking very loudly, and they were convinced everything they said was really funny, and they were spouting off all kinds of crap, and they were falling down a lot. Then a kindly woodcutter happened to be passing by and he heard their shouts of "I'm not drrrrunk! You're drunk! Why I oughta punch your lights out!" The woodcutter rushed in, killed the witch, rescued Hansel and Gretel, and got them a movie deal.

MORAL OF THE STORY: You need professional help. But young people don't see any relevance.

POSSUM LODGE MEETINGS

Every month the Possum Lodge membership meets to discuss important issues. These meetings are glimpsed at the end of each episode of "The Red Green Show" and the new Red Green show, which I call "The New Red Green Show." Many of you have written and asked, "What is with those meetings?"

To satisfy the curiosity of all of you, and probably nauseate more than a few of you, here's a complete transcript of one of our lodge meetings. I trust none of you will ever ask again.

HAROLD: All rise! (EVERYONE RISES)
ALL: (MORE OR LESS TOGETHER) Quando Omni Flunkus Moritati.
RED: Be seated. Is there any old business or new business or future business? No? Then I move this meeting be closed and the bar be opened...
HAROLD: Uncle Red, several members have their hands up. Including myself.
RED: (PAUSE) Alright. Stinky, what's wrong?
STINKY: Thanks Red. I move that we sell that thing out behind the lodge.
RED: Which thing is that? There must be five thousand things out there. Could you narrow it down a bit?
STINKY: The big ugly thing... (SILENCE) The one that smells bad... The one that's all broken and rusted... and no use to anyone.
RED: Does anyone know which thing he means?
JUNIOR: It's that big blue and gray thing. The abandoned hulk of a truck of some kind.
RED: That's my Possum van.
STINKY: The thing I'm talking about has a long thing coming out the top. Like a metal thing.
OLD MAN SEDGWICK: That's my iron lung! I'm saving that for my retirement.
STINKY: No, not the lung.
JUNIOR: That's not there anymore.
O.M. SEDGWICK: What? Who took it?
RED: Uh, some burglars made off with it a few weeks back.
HAROLD: Are you sure Uncle Red?
RED: Shutup Harold.
HAROLD: I don't think burglars stole it.
RED: Yes, they did.
HAROLD: No, I'm pretty sure it wasn't stolen. I think a member took it.
O.M. SEDGWICK: What? I'll skin 'em alive!
HAROLD: Yes, I'm sure someone here took it. Now who was it? Let me think.

RED: Don't think, Harold.

HAROLD: They were going to make it into something... Why would they have told me? Oh, I remember. It was going to be made into a submarine by someone....

RED: Shutup Harold....

HAROLD: Oh, that's right. It was for Handyman Corner with Unc... Oh...Uh. Actually, Mr. Sedgwick, yes, it was stolen by burglars.

O.M. SEDGWICK: What's the world coming to? It's them young people. Buncha punks. Kids today! Got no brains. Got no morals.

RED: Thank you, Old Man Sedgwick, can we get back to the business at hand?

O.M. SEDGWICK: Oh sure. Who cares about me? You know in Japan, older people are revered for their wisdom.

BUSTER: Well how about we pass around the hat and buy you a one-way ticket to Tokyo?

O.M. SEDGWICK: I heard that! I heard that!

BUSTER: Of course you heard that. I shouted it right in your face.

O.M. SEDGWICK: What? What did he say? Oh forget it. You pip-squeaks. You just want to get rid of me. Well I ain't going!

RED: I want to get to the business at hand.

STINKY: Yeah. I want to sell the ugly old thing no one wants any more.

O.M. SEDGWICK: I said I ain't going.

ALL: Shutup! SHUTUP! SHUTUP!

O.M. SEDGWICK: I heard that. ZZZZZZZZZZZ

RED: Oh good. He's fallen asleep. Now what is this thing you're talking about Stinky?

STINKY: The orange cylinder thing with the black end.

BUSTER: The old septic tank?

STINKY: No.

JUNIOR: I'm saving that septic tank. I'm going to make it into a big lawn roller.

RED: Actually, I had my eye on it for a tree fort for Harold.

HAROLD: Eww. Gross. How would you get the stink and smell out of it?

RED: I'd say "Harold, come down for dinner." (RAUCOUS LAUGHTER)

HAROLD: Shutup! Shutup! Everyone shutup, or you'll wake Old Man Sedgwick. (SUDDEN SILENCE)

STINKY: The thing I'm talking about is behind the broken back hoe, just past the airplane tailfin, beside the stack of broken fence posts, and the huge ball of string.

RED: My giant electric pencil?

STINKY: Not that far back.

BUSTER: He means the wheels off that old railway car.

STINKY: No, it's just beside that.

JUNIOR: My sculpture?

STINKY: Sculpture?

JUNIOR: Yeah. I made that out of an old earth moving machine. I cut it into pieces and reassembled it into a work of art.

STINKY: I don't know about art, but I know what I like. And I like getting money for scrap metal.

JUNIOR: It's art!

STINKY: It's an eyesore.

JUNIOR: That's because it's modern art.

RED: Well Junior, have you considered converting your creation
into a piece of kinetic art?

JUNIOR: Kinn... Huhn? What's that?

HAROLD: Oh, I know Uncle Red. Kinetic art is artwork that
includes movement. This brings the elements of time and
motion into the work.

JUNIOR: Oh yeah?

RED: Movement would increase the value of the art.

JUNIOR: Yeah?

RED: Yeah.

JUNIOR: Okay!

RED: Great. Okay, Stinky, move it over to the scrap dealer.

STINKY: Right Red.

JUNIOR: No! You're not touching my work of art.

HAROLD: Uh, Junior, I mean Mr. Singleton, it may be art, but it's
badly done and it doesn't look like anything. It doesn't
even have a title.

JUNIOR: Yes, it does. "Two Reclining Nude Women." (SILENCE)

BUSTER: Wow. Man, that's a great work of art.

STINKY: I think we should move it to the front of the lodge.

HAROLD: I love it. I could look at it for hours.

RED: Okay, any other business? Yes Moose?

MOOSE: Ahem... Ahem... Ahem... Ahhhhhhhemmm. Ahem. Ahem.
Ahhhhhem. ArrrgghhhhhaaaaahHHHHHheemmm! (COUGH COUGH) Ahem.
(Throat clearing) Ahem, ahem.... Sorry. I just wanted to
say, we can learn a lot from studying animals, but never
never never try to clean yourself the way a cat does.
Ahem... Ahem. (COUGH COUGH) Ahemmmm....

RED: Thanks Moose. Any other hairballs of wisdom from anyone
else?

HAROLD: Yes, several viewers have written asking how come Bill
never talks in the "Adventures with Bill" or any other part
of the show. People figure it's some kind of conspiracy.
Like maybe Bill has a weird voice so he's not allowed to
talk.

RED: Nonsense. We allow you to talk, Harold.

HAROLD: True... Hey!?...

RED: Well Harold, write 'em back and tell those people Bill does
talk. All the time. Right Bill? (BILL NODS)
The reason they don't hear Bill talk is because that old
black & white movie camera doesn't have a very good
microphone. Right Bill? (BILL NODS)
And if Bill wants to talk, he's more than welcome to. Right
Bill?

BILL: Sure Red. You betcha. Yes sir. If I have anything to say.

Not that I do right now. I mean when there's something to say, you can bet I'll say it. As my daughter Marsha says—Marsha is our oldest, she's off at Trent University now, studying forestry. First year. She's in her first year. I mean her first year at forestry. She's not in her first year. They don't allow one-year-olds into university. Even at Trent. She's a freshman. Or a freshwoman. She's a freshperson. Maybe she's a sophomore. Marsha's studying forestry. She's going to be a forester. Go round foresting and stuff. Not the biggest salaries in the world, you know, making a career in foresting. The real money is in de-foresting. Logging. That's where the mega-money is, but my daughter, Marsha, she's our oldest, she couldn't look herself in the face if she did de-foresting. She wouldn't be able to look herself in the face. Speaking of not being able to look herself in the face, our youngest, Tammy, she's had her teeth fixed! The bottom ones point up now, and the top ones point down! Beauuuutiful. Those top teeth of hers are perfectly aligned now. They're perfectly parallel. Both of 'em. Now if we could just get Milton to go to the orthodontist. Milton's our middle one. You know what they say about the middle child. Middle's child is full of Woah! Like when he fell off the chimney he yelled, "Woah!" A chip off the old block that one. Good kid really. Good with his hands. Yes sir, he's real good with his hands. And not so good without his hands. When he had those casts on his hands, after that accident with our barbecue, he was no good at all. Couldn't hold a spoon or a cup. But he tried. I'll give him that. Never say die. That's my Milton. He never said die. His mother and I said it sometimes, but he didn't. But then he didn't have to clean up the food he kept dropping. Still, he's got the casts off and he's doing great. Got his own... (INDETERMINATE TIME PASSAGE. The tape recorder ran out of tape, and the guy operating it had fallen asleep, as had everyone else.)

MUCH LATER...

BILL: ...and Grandma found the lump of peameal bacon in our laundry hamper. But by then it was rotten. And to make a long story short, that's when Marsha decided to study forestry at Trent. And Tammy decided to get her teeth fixed.

RED: (YAWN) Thank you Bill. Anything else? No? Then the meeting is closed and the bar is open.

ALL: Here, here! Seconded! Yaayyy!

HAROLD: Wait! It's two in the morning. It's too late. The cash bar is closed. (ANGRY SHOUTS, CURSES, THREATS)

HAROLD: It's not my fault! That's the law! Stop it! Oh, real nice! Same to you! ....Ouch! Who threw that?! Don't... hey! Oww! Let go of my... Owwwww!

RED: No guys. Settle down. Harold's right. We can't sell beer this late.

ALL: Awwww.

RED: So it's free.

ALL: Yayyyyy! (GENERAL STAMPEDE UPSTAIRS, TWENTY MINUTES OF SILENCE)

O.M. SEDGWICK: Huhn! What? Was I sleeping? Did I miss anything?

THE SURPRISING NUTRITIONAL VALUE OF JUNK FOOD

You Are What You Eat

When I was a kid there was no such thing as Health Food because back then all food was pretty healthy. Today, thanks to the breakthroughs in food preparation technology, we can eat a three-course meal that is about 2,394 steps removed from a farm. In fact, many of our modern snack foods are leftover by-products from the manufacture of synthetic upholstery.

Generally speaking, a fast-food snack with a name like "Cheez-O-Rinos" has virtually nothing to do with cheese. Some consumers feel this is false advertising, whereas in fact the name on the package quite clearly states that it contains Cheez, not cheese. The fact that "Cheez" is the industrial term for a waste chemical that's skimmed off vats of latex house paint is never mentioned by the food company.

When you check on the nutritional value of snacks like "Cinnamon Whizzeys," "Choco-Drips," or "Gribble Grabble," you'll find the label on the cellophane package usually says something like... "each 10 oz. serving contains the recommended annual intake of salt, Vitamin L, and Di-ethyl-methyl-ketone. Uranium added to preserve freshness."

If you are going to hoover down a lot of junk food, your heart certainly doesn't deserve the extra strain that comes from worrying about what you've just inhaled. So when some health nut teases you because you've just knocked back a party-size bag of "Ketchup Flavoured Tater-rinos" and a gallon of "Zap" cola for breakfast, pull out this handy chart which proves that snack foods are good, and good for you.

PRETZELS: Pretzels are an excellent source of fibre and salt. Also the pretzel shape helps get between teeth and clean them.

SOUR CREAM & ONION POTATO CHIPS: This snack is basically a complete well-balanced meal. It includes all of the four basic food groups:

1. Dairy—sour cream!
2. Fruit & Veg—Onions!
3. Grains—Potatoes!
4. Meats—The little bits of coloured green stuff!

BOSTON CREAM DOUGHNUTS: This is another well-balanced food. The custardy-yellow centre provides you with the recommended daily intake of dairy and sugar. If it's artificial, then you're getting soybean oil which is also good for you. The doughnut fills you with fibre and sugar, while the chocolate glaze gives you energy and sugar. And if it's a sugar doughnut, it gives you extra energy.

FRENCH FRIES WITH GRAVY AND KETCHUP: Recommended for those who don't always get enough vegetables. The fries are potatoes; the ketchup is made of two kinds of vegetables—tomatoes and sugar cane; and the gravy is basically vegetable oil or soybean oil. The thicker gravy is rich in Vitamins and Ribald-flavin.

JELLY BEANS: Another great source of energy. The red food colouring helps keep your complexion looking pink, while the hard candy coating on the jelly beans is essential for strong nails and shiny hair. A big bowl of green jelly beans is as good for you as a big bowl of green beans.

PEZ: Pez builds strong bones. And loading the Pez into the dispenser helps develop fine motor skills and hand-eye coordination.

CHEWING GUM: Builds strong jaw muscles, cleans bits of potato chips from your teeth, freshens your breath, and the little Bazooka Joe comic encourages literacy amongst our young people.

```
peanut butter
You hear a lot of talk about spinach and soy
And which one makes the perfect supper
But when it comes to that I'll tell you boy
You can't beat peanut butter
Easy to cut and easy to chew
Never goes hard as a rock
It's the one and only food
So good it made Mister Ed talk
```

Never eat things that move.

YOU TOO CAN COOK

NEVER COOKED A THING IN YOUR LIFE?
(EXCEPT THE BOOKS AT YOUR COMPANY)

HERE'S EVERYTHING YOU NEED TO SERVE A DELICIOUS SIX-COURSE FEAST
THAT WILL DRIVE YOUR FAMILY FROM SOUP TO NUTS!

FIRST COURSE: HORS D'OEUVRES

Serated Pommes de Terre & Creamy Vegetable Dip.

SERVES: 1 - 6

INGREDIENTS:

      1 Bag of rippled potato chips

      1 Tub of chip dip

STEPS: 1. Carefully open cellophane bag using scissors, serated knife, or teeth.

        2. Pour chips into a serving bowl. Serve at room temperature.

        3. Remove chip dip from fridge, grab tab on metal lid, peel outer edge of lid, pry back lid and remove—save lid for storing any leftover dip.

        4. Pour off any oil on the top of the dip and serve.

SECOND COURSE: SALAD

Caesar Salad

SERVES: 1 - 6 hungry people

INGREDIENTS:

      Lettuce, the long green leafy kind, not the round balled up heavy kind.

      1 Raw Egg

      1/2 cup oil (olive or 10-W-30)

      4 cloves garlic

      Dollop of Lemon Juice

      Large Handful of Parmesan Cheese

      Small Handful of Salt

      Dehydrated Anchovies (saved from an old pizza)

      OR

      1 Bottle of Caesar Salad dressing

STEPS: 1. Shred the salad using bare hands or chain saw.

        2. Wash the lettuce (Optional).

        3. Dry lettuce with blowdryer or in microwave oven.

        4. Pour dressing over salad.

        5. Put salad in bowl—actually, do this before you dump the salad dressing.

        6. Serve and stand back.

THIRD COURSE: SOUP

Hearty Traditional Vegetable Soup

SERVES: 1 - 4 desperate people

INGREDIENTS:

1 cup diced vegetables	1 cup water (tap or rain)
1 cup of salt	Butylayted Hydroxotoulene
Xanthan Gum	Mono-Sodium Glutamate
Food Colouring	Calcium Disodium EDTA
Propylene Glycol	Artificial Flavours
Modified Food Starch	Tapioca Dextrin
Milk Solids	Sorbic Acid
OR	
2 cans of soup	

STEPS: 1. Heat 1 can of soup in a pot until it explodes. There's your ambience.
   2. Get the second can, remove the lid, pour it into the pot and heat it properly.
   3. Pour in bowls and serve.

FOURTH COURSE: ENTREE

Noodles Au Gratin, French-Cut Beans & Tomato Croquets

SERVES: 1 - 4

INGREDIENTS:

Kraft Dinner	Can of French-cut beans
Tomatoes	Pickles

STEPS: 1. Make the Kraft Dinner according to the instructions on the little bag of cheese that comes with it.
2. Carefully open the can of beans and bring to a boil in a pot or right in the can.
3. Cut the middle out of each tomato, jam a pickle in the hole, microwave for one minute.
4. Serve on a plate with knife and fork.

FIFTH COURSE: DESSERT

Un-Baked Brandied Apples

SERVES: 1 - 8

INGREDIENTS:

8 Apples (as bruise-free as possible)	1 Cup Raisins
1 Cup Brown Sugar	4 tbsp cinnamon
32 oz Bottle of Brandy	3 oz. of Nutmeg

STEPS: 1. Serve the brandy.
2. After the brandy bottle is empty, set the apples, raisins, cinnamon, sugar and nutmeg out in bowls and let people chow down.

SIXTH COURSE: APERITIF

STEPS: 1. Order a pizza.

> *Only purchase an item from the person who made it. Unless you're buying manure.*

THE INCREDIBLE LIGHTNESS OF BEING UNATTRACTIVE

Over the years I've met a number of good-looking people and a whole lot of ugly ones, and I think the ugly people have more fun. The beautiful ones get people staring at them all the time, and giving them important jobs with responsibility, and always trying to have sex with them at various sporting events and hardware conventions. Whereas when you're ugly, nobody bothers you like that. And when you're good-looking everybody expects you to be stupid. Whereas when you're ugly, they assume you're smart and as long as you don't ever say or do anything, they'll keep that opinion. That's why most politicians are ugly. The only downside to being unattractive is the "pity factor." I don't want anybody feeling sorry for me because I'm not handsome. I look at it this way. No matter how good you look now, you're gonna be ugly some day. Look at anybody over a 100. That's how we're all gonna look. We're all gonna be ugly sometime in the future. Those of us who are ugly now are just mature beyond our years.

UNUSUAL WILDLIFE AT POSSUM LAKE

THE SILVER-TUFTED WALKER

A robin-sized bird that travels everywhere on foot. Eats twigs, leaves, small coins and previously-enjoyed gum. Mates in the spring and has a very short lifespan because it walks south for the winter. Often picked up for loitering, especially around Thanksgiving. A strange bird that sees extinction as a strategic career move. Never flies. Afraid of heights.

THE PURPLE-CRESTED SIDING-PECKER

Similar to a woodpecker, this bird prefers to hammer on aluminum siding. Obviously deaf. And not too smart. Only one example of this unusual species was ever seen around Possum Lake. It preferred the aluminum siding on Buster's lime-green tool shed. It tried to mate with the bird on my aluminum windvane and nested in my aluminum eavestrough for 5 years, until it flew head first into an aluminum window. Tasted great when cooked in my aluminum pot.

THE AMPHICARP

Growing to between two feet and sixty feet, depending on who's telling the story, the Amphicarp resembles a large goldfish with the exception of the antenna-shaped dorsal fin tuned to a local soft-rock FM station, and the set of miniature wheels protruding from the chest and stomach. As a bottom feeder, the fish uses the wheels effectively, particularly when parallel parking. On land it gets well over 30 miles to the gallon. The first and only Amphicarp was biologically engineered during an unfortunate high-impact mating session between a carp and a radio-controlled dune buggy. Although there is some hope of catching the Amphicarp once the batteries wear down, to date it remains "the one that sped away."

THE BARF SNAKE

Named after Ralph Barf because of the striking physical resemblance. The Barf Snake moves by lying on the ground and rolling over sideways, as did Ralph on his way home from office parties. Although they prefer flat surfaces like sidewalks and ranch-style homes, they are often seen up against speed bumps, catching their breath. Natural enemies: cats, really hungry birds and steam rollers.

ICE FISHING HINTS

STEP 1.   Do this activity in the winter. No kidding.

STEP 2.   Learn how to hot-wire a snowmobile.

STEP 3.   Hot-wire a snowmobile and send the least
popular guy out on the lake. Chances are
he will sink through the ice
and drop like a stone to the
bottom. DO NOT
ATTEMPT TO FISH IN
THE RESULTANT
HOLE. THAT'S
IMPORTANT.
Instead, go to
a different
lake before the cops arrive and you waste the
whole day explaining how it happened.

STEP 4.   Hot-wire another, nicer
snowmobile and go out onto a
safer lake. Hold up a three-foot
length of 4-inch pipe and stick
the bottom end into the ice. Fill
the pipe with gasoline and light
it. In no time at all, you will have
a four-inch hole in the ice. If you
park your snowmobile too close
to the burning pipe, you will end
up with an even bigger hole and
an interesting story to tell all the
nurses at the burn unit.

STEP 5.   Bait your hook and drop it into the hole.
Try not to think about your feet until they are
completely numb. If you have a chainsaw, you
can cut a trough in the ice and troll. Otherwise
you're pretty well limited to jerking the line up
and down and letting your mind wander. DO
NOT FIGHT THE BOREDOM. IT IS AN
INTRINSIC COMPONENT OF THE SPORT.

STEP 6.   If you catch anything other than pneumonia, you may need help reeling it in. Especially if it's thicker than four inches. Many of today's sophisticated fishing reels are not meant to be operated with frozen fingers so thaw your fingers by putting them in your mouth, unless you really don't like the taste of bait. Once you've landed the fish, stick them face down in the snow until frozen. This will eliminate the need for a stringer as you can mount the fish on popsicle sticks and throw them into your cooler.

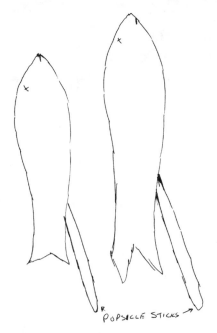

POPSICLE STICKS

STEP 7.   Once you're back to the cabin, cover the fish in a light coating of bread crumbs and butter and then fry them up in a quart and a half of Scotch. Take them out of the pan and feed them to the cat while you drink the broth. This will remove all memory of the outing and will allow you to go ice fishing on another occasion.

```
ICE FISHING
   By Red Green
It is winter.
Wind whips across the frozen lake
But a lone figure drags a wooden shed across the ice.
The ice fisherman.
He stops in a clear spot and goes into his shed.
Then he struggles and groans to drill down
     through the creaking ice.
Finally he lowers a line.
Sitting in his little dark shed for hours.
Waiting for a nibble.
That lone figure gives us all hope.
Because you realize your home life can't be anywhere
     near as bad as his.
```

MEET YOUR MEMBER.

Okay, time now to meet the man who repairs all the cars and trucks and combinations of both around Possum Lodge. He knows everything there is to know about racing cams and compression ratios and how it feels to be upside down in a vehicle. He says he's in love with his huge monster truck, although he has had a crush on several used Grenadas.

DOUGIE FRANKLIN

FULL NAME: Dougie Franklin

AGE: I was born in 1953, the same year the first Corvettes came out.

OCCUPATION: Master Mechanic and Monster Truck a-fitchy-an-ado.

MARITAL STATUS: Previously Owned, Make An Offer.

HOBBIES: Trucks. Cars. Vehicles. Anything with engines.

MAJOR TURN ONS: Trucks. Cars. Vehicles. Anything with engines.

MAJOR TURN OFFS: Speed limits. Load limits. Oncoming traffic. Crash helmets that can't take a beating.

FAVOURITE COLOUR: Metal-flake candy-apple red.

FAVOURITE FOOD: Red candy apples. Anything I can buy at a drive-thru.

FAVOURITE MOVIES: "Death Race 2000". "Monster Truck Bloopers 2" (That's me driving the van that catches fire and explodes. Fame is fleeting.)

FAVOURITE BOOKS: "Chilton's Auto Guides". "The Constitution Of The United States". "Richie Rich" comics. (That kid kills me.)

PROUDEST ACCOMPLISHMENT: Living with all these Canadians and not killing any of 'em. Oh yeah, and the flaming-van-that-exploded incident.

LODGE RESPONSIBILITIES: Keeping everyone's car running. And dispensing hard-earned nuggets of wisdom about yer fairer sex.

MEET YOUR MEMBER.

Okay, time now to meet the man who sells all the marine equipment on Possum Lake. He recommends you always buy the best 'cause if you buy a cheap boat and it breaks down, don't come to him. When the Statue of Liberty said, "Bring me your tired and your hungry" she must have meant this guy because he does nothing but sleep and eat.

GLEN BRACKSTON

FULL NAME: Glen Oliver Brackston.

AGE: 32. Same as my waistline. Not inches.

OCCUPATION: Owner/operator Brackston's Marina.

MARITAL STATUS: Married with 7 daughters.

HOBBIES: No time for hobbies, what with running my marina and raising 7 daughters and fishing and hanging out with my friends and watching TV and collecting coins.

MAJOR TURN ONS: Vacations. Naps. Sick days. My Recreational vehicle.

MAJOR TURN OFFS: Boats and marinas. Seeing food going to waste. Heart attacks where you have to stay in the hospital for a few days and eat hospital food. Type-A personalities. Grade B meats.

FAVOURITE COLOUR: Aquamarine. I'm painting my RV aquamarine. It's gonna look so great.

FAVOURITE FOOD: Second helpings. Midnight snacks.

FAVOURITE MOVIES: "7 Brides For 7 Brothers". "My Left Foot". (I really admired a guy who could do all that without getting up.)

FAVOURITE BOOKS: I prefer those books on cassette. You don't have to hold them up so your arms don't get tired.

PROUDEST ACCOMPLISHMENT: My seven beautiful daughters. And surviving two heart attacks.

LODGE RESPONSIBILITIES: Selling boats to the guys. After that they're on their own.

QUALITY TIME

It's always a good thing for a father to spend time with his child in some activity or sport or a police chase. Many lifelong memories are created during those special times when Dad and the little one head out for a day at the Museum of Natural History and find themselves hopelessly lost in a discount mall. However there are a few guidelines that you should know that can help you spend a day with your offspring without getting totally off-sprung.

First off, pick an activity that you really like to do. Despite their cute protests, all kids secretly love to go fishing. They just don't know it. They may want to go to a theme park or a gang war of some kind, but they can do that on their own time and besides, what do they know? Whatever you decide to do, get an early start—4:30 a.m. is a good target. That way your son or daughter will want to come home early before your relationship starts to deteriorate.

Okay, now it's important that this also be an educational experience for the child so make sure there's lots of chances to learn as much as possible. Like how to carry stuff, and how to make a comfortable seat for both of you, and how to run and get things that you may ask for

throughout the duration of the fun. Children learn by doing. And by fetching. And by lifting.

After you've arrived and one of you has made 27 trips back to the car to get something and you have everything set up and have assembled all of your fishing gear and have set your lines and have made yourselves comfortable, and there's nothing left to do but enjoy the day, PACK EVERYTHING UP AND GO HOME. This is very important. The only enjoyable part of the outing—i.e. the anticipation—is now over and you have entered the dangerous part of the adventure—i.e. the reality.

Reality never matches the anticipation. After all, what child ever anticipated arguing, fighting, insulting, getting cold, hungry, grumpy, catching nothing, finding the boat leaks and sinking in ice cold water? If you don't have the courage to pack up and go home, you will see the following behaviour pattern developing, which will be difficult for you to handle.

PHASE ONE: The Twitch

Remember, children can't sit still. They start asking annoying questions about the sky. They keep fiddling with the fishing rod. They want to try a sip of whatever it is in your flask that you keep drinking. They mention their favourite cartoon show that they'd be watching if they were home right now. Then your child, the same one who can't remember to shut the screen door or pick up clothes, will describe in intimate detail all 214 levels of some video game, including what you have to do to get past each level and the maximum number of points you can earn on each level and the highest scores that they and every one of their friends have ever gotten. You will find yourself

WORMS
By Red Green

Spring has hit the
    city
There's leaves on
    every tree
And worms festoon
    the sidewalks
As far as the eye
    can see
Trampled under
    boots and heels
They're flatter
    than Bobby Vee
At the Lodge the
    worms are luckier
They get to go
    fishing with me

confused over whether Mario and Luigi are pals or games or a rap group.

PHASE TWO: The Placation

To hold the child's attention, you serve lunch. Even though it's 8 a.m. They don't like anything except the cookies which they accidentally drop in the river. They turn their nose up at the huge baloney, ham, beef, peanut butter sandwiches you made. They open a can of pop all over you and then fall on the sandwiches, knocking them down into the oil-filled bottom of the boat, giving the sandwiches such a horrible taste that you can hardly keep them down. They start crying and other fishermen move away from the area. You envy the other fishermen. Finally your child settles down, grows quiet and peaceful and then suddenly vomits right into the minnow pail.

PHASE THREE: The Confrontation

The child starts to imply that the adventure is over. They have packed up all their stuff. They ask if they can sit in the car and read maps. You tell them that if they want to go home, they should just say so. They just say so. You say, "Was that a wolf I saw on the shore?" They stare at the shore for about ten minutes before realizing you were lying. They start whining about going home. You argue for a few minutes. You put your foot down and they pout. After two minutes the pouting is driving you nuts and scaring the fish away. You start to wish there was a wolf on the shore. You wind in your line, making a lot of noise and acting real disappointed. You get a nibble. You ignore it.

PHASE FOUR: The Silence

On the drive home your thoughts are not interrupted by any conversation or movement as the child sits quietly and stares out the window. About a block from your house the child puts a hand on your shoulder and thanks you for a great day and says, "Can't wait to tell Mom about everything we did." When you get in the door, the child regales your wife with stories of wolves, oil sandwiches and throwing up in the bait pail. Your wife nods and smiles at the child, then quietly tells you she'll never understand the attraction of fishing.

PHASE FIVE: The Revelation

You find yourself leafing through a Disneyworld brochure.

HOCKEY
By Red Green
It is winter.
When I was young
we never had fights
in hockey.
But we also never
had helmets.
Or protective pads.
Or shields on our
skate blades
Or smooth ice.
We used broken
splintered sticks
And a brick for a
puck.
And big hard rocks
for the posts.
But we never had
fights.
We didn't need
fights.

*You can lead a horse to water,
but you can't make him pass it.*

POSSUM LODGE PARTY GAMES

"BECAUSE NOTHING LIVENS UP A PARTY LIKE HAVING TO CALL THE RIOT SQUAD."

TREASURE HUNT

When you're at someone's house and they're busy in the kitchen with some type of fire, pry off one of their furnace vents and drop in a really old egg. Replace the vent and wait for the fun to start. The game is over when somebody finds the egg or the guests pass out or the hostess insists it's time for Grandpa to see a specialist.

DOGGY, DOGGY WHO'S GOT THE BONE?

Everyone sits in a circle or an ellipse, depending on the room's shape. One contestant leaves the room and, while they're gone, one of the people in the circle consumes 7 or 8 martinis in as many minutes. The contestant returns to the room and tries to guess who had the drinks. They are allowed to check your breath for a trace of olives, or you might be asked to perform a motor skill, or sing one of the uptempo numbers from *Mary Poppins*. Although the first round is pretty obvious, the game gets more difficult as the evening progresses. The game is over when you run out of martinis, or the paramedics arrive.

PUBLISHER'S NOTE: Do not under any circumstances ever play this game.

CHAINSAW PUZZLE

Exactly like a jigsaw puzzle. Well not exactly. Instead of a jigsaw, you use a chainsaw to make the puzzle. And instead of a puzzle of some Mediterranean village, you saw up an old chair, a broken freezer, or a used car. And you don't bother putting it back together—that's boring. And there's usually one piece missing at the end, but it's usually a piece of someone who stood too close.

EGO PURSUIT

Get out one of the popular trivia games and divide the players into teams. Play the game as per the instructions with the teams taking turns asking each other questions. The game is played exactly as explained by the manufacturer with one important difference—ALL ANSWERS WILL BE ACCEPTED AS CORRECT.

Example: Team 1: Who was the 23rd President of the United States?
                Team 2: Colonel Saunders.
                Team 1: Correct.

      OR   Team 2: What is the name of the fifth planet from the Sun?
                Team 1: Stan.
                Team 2: Right on!

Each team is also obliged to compliment the answer.

Example: Team 1: What is the main ingredient in Hollandaise?
                Team 2: Holland.
                Team 1: Yes! Good work! Excellent! Wow, you sure know stuff. Do you have a BA in general arts?

The winner is the team that ends up feeling the best about themselves.

HAROLD SPEAKS.

Okay. Tolerating Relatives. Okay my relatives came over last weekend. Now a wise man once said, "You can pick your friends and you can pick your nose, but you can't pick your relatives." That's intuitive. I know. I've lived it. Everyone saying, "My how you've grown. And hasn't your skin cleared up." It's like humiliating. The abuse, the insults. The people pinching and grabbing at you.

So now I've found a way to get back at 'em. I'm even more obnoxious than they are. No really, I can do it. Like when they say how tall I am, I say, "Have you shrunk?" And I say, "My how you've grown in the stomach area." Or "Haven't we gone grayer!" Or "Are you still alive, Grandma?"

And then of course I'm excused to get on with my life and hang out at the mall with my friends. Well okay, my friend. Thank you.

ROLLING A SNOWMAN
By Red Green

It is Winter
The young children
   are busy rolling a
   snowman on the
   front lawn
While the teenagers
   are busy rolling a
   drunk in the park.

FIGURE SKATING
By Red Green

We're skating on the
   pond.
And Moose Thompson
   does a triple axle,
   followed by a
   quadruple Lutz and
   a triple toe loop.
That's what happens
   when you're on a
   breakaway
And you catch your
   toe on a frozen
   weasel.

Real men don't need cutlery.

WATCH FOR MORE GREAT POSSUM LODGE GAMES:

Spin the Assault Weapon	Blindman's Buff
Tiddley Wanks	I Spy With My Little Nose
Turkey in the Trousers	Hide and Leave
Who's Shoes?	Hops 'n Scotch
Simon and Garfunkel Says Shoes	Pin the Tail on Someone Tying their
Follow The Leaper	Bust A Belly Button
Truth or Dave	Kick My Can
Thud that Dud Spud, Bud.	

Okay, time now to meet the man who flies his own bush plane all over Possum Lake and onto Possum Lake and even into Possum Lake.

Nobody knows how he got his piloting experience, but I would guess it was during a war of some kind and he was fighting for the side that had the least money. He says "Far out," and he is.

BUZZ SHERWOOD

FULL NAME: Kenneth Staples... something... something... I forget... Sherwood.

AGE: I was 19 at the first Woodstock Festival... so that makes me.... oh man. I'm old!

OCCUPATION: Rebel Without A Cause. Bush Pilot, CEO of Buzz Off Airlines. Stunt pilot. Whatever.

MARITAL STATUS: Married a bunch of times, but mostly by guys who weren't officially ministers. Presently I'm batching it. Or botching it.

HOBBIES: Life.

MAJOR TURN ONS: Fighting "The man." Doing something to save the planet. Trying to reach spiritual alignment. And blonde chicks.

MAJOR TURN OFFS: Anything after the Beatles broke up.

FAVOURITE COLOUR: Purple Haze.

FAVOURITE FOOD: Munchies.

FAVOURITE MOVIES: "Easy Rider".

FAVOURITE BOOKS: "Zen And The Art of Light Aircraft Maintenance". "The Kama Sutra". "Tintin in Tibet".

PROUDEST ACCOMPLISHMENT: Learning to "just say no," and not ending up as some kind of burnout from the '60s who can't even, you know, like do the, the whole thing with the... Did you know I dated Grace Slick? And if you listen to the Rolling Stones live version of "Midnight Rambler", the guy who screams near the end, that's me!

LODGE RESPONSIBILITIES: Air Rescue. Air Charter. Air Sickness.

Okay, time now to meet the man who is the largest living land mass in the Possum Lake area. Everything about this guy is big—input, output and central processor. His birth weight was 18 pounds, which was a record for a preemie. Everybody gets along with him because that's the only intelligent thing to do with a guy whose thumb is bigger than your face.

MOOSE THOMPSON

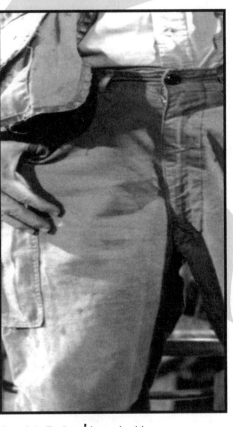

FULL NAME: Mooseworth Hugo Largess Thompson

AGE: 29

OCCUPATION: Part time bouncer. Studying to be a veterinary chiropractor.

MARITAL STATUS: I've yet to meet a woman who comes up to my high standards. Or my navel.

HOBBIES: Eating.

MAJOR TURN ONS: Lifting heavy things. Punching big things. Smashing huge things.

MAJOR TURN OFFS: Low doorways. Narrow doorways. In fact most doorways. Flimsy furniture. Any joke about big dumb guys, especially if I don't get it.

FAVOURITE COLOUR: Pizza.

FAVOURITE FOOD: Bulk stuff

FAVOURITE MOVIES: The free videotape where Suzanne Somers demonstrates the Thighmaster.

FAVOURITE BOOKS: How do you mean?

PROUDEST ACCOMPLISHMENT: The time I ate a sandwich that was larger than Old Man Sedgwick.

LODGE RESPONSIBILITIES: Lifting heavy things. Punching big things. Smashing huge things.

TEEN TALK

Last week my wife found some old photos of me when I was a teenager. Yes, they had photography back then. Golly, the way I dressed, the way I combed my hair, the shoes I wore. It was pretty scary stuff. I thought, well, at least I look sharp these days.

My only real consolation is that 15 or 20 years from now when today's teenagers see pictures of themselves as kids they're gonna be even more humiliated. Picture some future vice-president of IBM passing around a photo of himself as a teenager, with a purple mohawk, cutlery for earrings, a dragon tattoo on his exposed stomach and jeans so baggy he's got room in the crotch for a family of groundhogs.

So if you've got a kid who looks like an extra from *Road Warrior*, snap lots of pictures of him. Then when he wises up and gets respectable you can sell him back the negatives... one at a time. Beats having to save your own money for retirement.

```
WINTER SURPRISE
   By Red Green
I toboggan in the bitter cold
The whole afternoon.
Then I stagger indoors to the warmth of the fire
As I peel off my parka and boots a white frozen
   lump falls out of my toque and skitters across
   the floor.
Is it a snow ball? A lump of ice? A pine cone?
Golly no, it's my left ear.
I think I'll go paint something
Perhaps the shed
```

TODAY'S STREET SLANG

Or how to understand what the heck your kids are saying about you.

I know we have a lot of fans amongst the younger generation X & Y chromosomes. In talking with them, I've learned a lot of their teenage lingo. Here's a dictionary of today's slang—learn these '90s phrases and you'll be a hep-cat like me, Daddy-O!

WORD	MEANING	WORD	MEANING
RAD	Good	BOGUS	Bad
GNARLY	Good	HAROLD	Bad
WAY GNARLY	Good	TOAST	Bad
JAMMIN'	Good	SCROAT	Bad
EXCELLENT	Good	DOOFUS	Bad
AWESOME	Good	DUUUH!	Bad
BAD	Good	GOOD	Bad
GREAT	Good	OH, GREAT!	Bad
SPLEB	Good	HI!	Bad
BOON-FOGGING	Good	PERFECT	Bad
PUNTING	Good	ME TOO	Bad

real big dog

He was a real big dog, his name was Kong
Musta weighed three hundred pounds
One eye was blue and the other was gone
And he tended to do things in mounds
There wasn't a job that dog couldn't do
If you gave him the plans he'd build it
Till the time he darted across the road one night
Ran over a Suzuki Sidekick and killed it.

SAVING FACE

How often has this happened to you? You encounter a friend or acquaintance who inquires about your family, and you find yourself struggling to find a polite way of explaining that your spouse has run off with a stump puller. Here we show you the wrong way and the right way to smooth over these socially awkward moments. And all without telling a single little white lie!

AWKWARD SITUATION #1

INCORRECT:

> FRIEND: "How's that son of yours doing?"
>
> YOU: "He's in prison for armed robbery."

CORRECT:

> FRIEND: "How's that son of yours doing?"
>
> YOU: "He's with the government. Full time. Department of Correctional Services. Got his own office. And they've guaranteed him at least 7 years."

AWKWARD SITUATION #2

INCORRECT:

> FRIEND: "How's your wonderful wife?"
>
> YOU: "She ran off with my best friend."

CORRECT:

> FRIEND: "How's your wonderful wife?"
>
> YOU: "Great. In all the time I've known her she hasn't been happier. She's just full of fun and finally enjoying life."

AWKWARD SITUATION #3

INCORRECT:

> FRIEND: "So how are things at work?"
>
> YOU: "I was fired so they could make a profit."

CORRECT:

> FRIEND: "So how are things at work?"
>
> YOU: "Great. The place is finally making a profit. And I was the one who made the difference."

HAROLD SPEAKS.

Okay. Modern Pressures. Okay, young people today are under a lot of pressure that our parents didn't have to think about, like war... okay, you had war, but sex, well I guess you had sex, or as you used to call it, love, but okay we have to worry about jobs, oh, right you had the Depression, but okay, peer pressure to do dangerous things, like I guess you had that too, okay, uh, did I say war? Did you guys have exams?

I know: what kind of skateboard to buy. And that puts a lot of pressure on us. And it hurts our heads and sometimes we want to scream and just go wild, but we don't. 'Cause everyone stares and you'll get thrown off the bus.

Anyway, I'm glad I got this off my chest. And I'm glad I wasn't born when you guys were. It must have been real boring. Thank you.

```
THE DARE
   By Red Green
It is winter.
The guys got drunk and put up cash
And I was the unfortunate one chosen
I won by running naked across the lake
But now my assets are frozen
```

AWKWARD SITUATION #4

INCORRECT:

FRIEND: "You look different. Did you get a haircut?"

YOU: "No, I put on twenty pounds, went on a nine-week bender, fell down drunk and broke my nose."

CORRECT:

FRIEND: "You look different. Did you get a haircut?"

YOU: "Yep."

AWKWARD SITUATION #5

INCORRECT:

FRIEND: "How's your father-in-law?"

YOU: "Nasty, stupid, rude, ignorant, bossy, unclean, overbearing, insensitive and unpleasant."

CORRECT:

FRIEND: "How's your father-in-law?"

YOU: "Same as always."

AWKWARD SITUATION #6

INCORRECT:

FRIEND: "So, what's new with your grandfather?"

YOU: "He's stone dead."

CORRECT:

FRIEND: "So, what's new with your grandfather?"

YOU: "Oh, you know… he can't complain. He's out of that old folks home he hated so much. And the kids seem to like him a lot more lately."

NORTH OF 40

I wanna say a few words to the middle-aged guys out there. I know what you're goin' through. I know what it's like to wake up two hours before your body does. Or to watch a full head of old hair swirl down the shower drain while a bushel of new hair sprouts out your nose and ears. Or when nature calls, you're never sure if it's gonna shout or whine or just whisper. Slippin' into the washroom is like goin' to a fireworks display. You stand there for what seems like an hour and a half before anything happens, then when it starts you're amazed, and you oooh and ahh, and you're never exactly sure when it's over.

And I know that a hearty meal of spicy food can turn into either a suicide attempt or murder, depending on whether or not you're alone in the car.

But it's all part of gettin' older. Oscar Wilde said, "Youth is wasted on the young," but I'll tell you at this point pretty near everything is wasted on me.

Still, I'm going to hang in there. I don't like growing old, but it sure beats the alternative. Remember, I'm pulling for ya 'cause we're all in this together.

There's only one thing worse than a sore loser, and that's Moose Thompson.

WHAT MAKES MEN DIFFERENT FROM WOMEN?

That's the $3,100 Question

Not all of the differences between the sexes are simply to do with fashion, haircuts and male oppression. As even the most ardent feminist will agree, men are physically different from women. And as the French say, "Vive la difference." Which translates as "I'll show you mine if you'll show me yours." (See now some women wouldn't find that funny. That's gotta be biological.)

According to scientists (real scientists, not just those actors wearing labcoats in the laxative commercials) women and men have physically different brains. More of a woman's brain is devoted to processing words, while men have more of the grey matter working on shapes and geometry. That's why men have trouble describing what they want and would rather just build it and if it's not right, throw it out. That's why they have trouble explaining what went wrong, whereas their wives seem to be able to name all kinds of stupid mistakes.

You can see the many areas where men are superior by studying their behavioural patterns.

1. *Men have better spatial sense than women.* For example, no woman would ever attempt to build a $3,100 garage without a level or a measuring tape simply because they can "eyeball it."

2. *Men have more sensitive eyesight than women.* For example, I can see all the things wrong with our old garage whereas my wife doesn't seem to notice any problems.

3. *Men are better drivers than women.* Especially with stuff like bulldozers, which we could use very easily to knock down the old garage if our wives would let us.

4. *Men are better at math.* For example, though my wife disagrees, I know that spending $3,100 to replace our garage, even though it has at least ten more years of life in it, actually makes economic sense in the long run considering interest rates and amortization and depreciation and good clean fun.

5. *Men are better at judging units of time.* For example, I can mentally calculate that even though the weekend is almost over, I could have our old garage torn down and the new one well under construction by sunset, and I'd finish it next week.

6. *Men are better at performing multiple tasks.* For example, even if I don't get the garage done next weekend, I'll do it along with the half-finished

boat, the half-finished trellis, the fence I started, the leaky bedroom ceiling I haven't finish patching, the toilet I haven't totally replaced, and the nine other jobs I have on the go.

7. *Men have better spatial projection abilities.* For example, I swear I can just picture how great a new garage would look, whereas my wife can't see what difference it would make.

8. *Men think more logically.* For example my wife thinks it's crazy to spend $3,100 and tear down a perfectly good garage, whereas I can see all the benefits and no matter how many times I explain them, she feels that having a brighter, cleaner place to store those old oil drums is not a major priority.

These are just the most obvious areas of male dominance that deserve scientific research or a study. I would be willing to undertake the study if someone gives me, say, $3,100.

This is only temporary, unless it works.

```
GROUND WIRE
   By Red Green
It is Winter
He stands by the chimney.
His cheeks and nose are rosy red
His whiskers are edged in white
Smoke curls from his mouth.
His suit is tinged with black soot.
I warned him to connect the ground wire before
   he plugged in the Christmas lights.
```

HAROLD SPEAKS.

Okay. Sex. Ha ha. Now that I have your attention I wanted to talk about driver education. There's something about driver education that really steams my clams.

Sex. Now that I have your attention again, I'd like to complain, 'cause I think that if you take one of these pro-driver courses to get a reduced insurance rate of under four thousand dollars a year, then you shouldn't have to learn with three students in the car.

Sex. Now that I have your attention again... I'm sure the last thing those other student drivers want is to have me in the back seat watching them drive over curbs, knock down signs and hit that stop sign. I sure hate it when I'm in the front. It's hard enough to concentrate on the road, sex, when you're driving and trying not to hit stuff, but how can you hear the instructor over the laughter? And the screaming. Sex. Thank you.

quiet affair

I often can guess how long they've been wed
By the volume at which they yell
The argument noise level goes up every year
After ten years you really can tell
He grunts and complains and starts up a fight
He bellows and roars like a bear
And likely as not she'll sneak off in the night
To go have a quiet affair

HOW TO SAVE YOUR MARRIAGE

"The couple that plays together, stays together."

The secret to a strong marriage is to share each other's interests. Or better still, to have her to share your interests. Now statistics show that a large percentage of women don't enjoy fishing. (And statistically women live longer than men, but I'm sure that's just a coincidence.)

So here are ten sure-fire "fishing lines" that will "lure" your spouse to get "hooked" on fishing. Good luck, "chum."

MOST EFFECTIVE

1. "Did you know fish oil can remove wrinkles from a person's skin? Scaling as few as five bass can make you look years younger."

2. "There's something really romantic about the sun rising on a lake in the middle of nowhere when it's freezing cold."

3. "Trolling for bass is all the rage in New York."

4. "Why is it that hipwaders make a person look fifteen pounds thinner?"

LESS EFFECTIVE

5. "If there are any minnows left over, you can dip them in lacquer and make beautiful earrings out of them."

6. "When I'm fishing, I don't talk."

7. "The kids won't be coming along."

LEAST EFFECTIVE

8. "Fishing could save us a bundle of money. I mean, it's free food! All we pay for is the gas, the bait, the beer, parking, the boat launching fee, lures, rods, and sunburn cream."

9. "Don't worry about bugs, the bats eat them."

10. "The great thing is you can go to the bathroom right over the side of the boat."

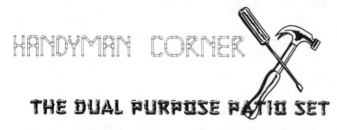

HANDYMAN CORNER

THE DUAL PURPOSE PATIO SET

Saving money is one of the main goals of all Lodge activities. As is finding money or even going through coat pockets in the cloakroom. It's hard to save money if you don't have any, so the next best thing is to save money by finding new ways to use things you already own. For example, if you have a home with a door and a couple of window awnings and a television antenna, you can make an attractive, cost-effective patio set. In the winter the house will look the way it does now; in the summer it will look quite different. Let's say you're starting with a house that looks like this:

Diagram A

From now on, this is how your house will look in the winter only.

Step One: Remove the television antenna. Nobody watches TV in the summer anyway. Now you could climb up on the roof to remove it, but it's very time-consuming to have to get the ladder back from the neighbour and climb all the way up there and then have to lie for an hour in the shrubs waiting for the ambulance. So I recommend you throw your boat anchor up onto the roof and try to hook it around the antenna pole. If you have a lot of anchor rope, you might want to clear the other side of the house of kids and lawn ornaments. Once you have the anchor hooked to the antenna, attach the other end of the rope to whichever one of your car bumpers has the least amount of rust. After you tie it on, bring the vehicle as close as possible to the house to create slack in the rope. (When removing a television antenna, you rely heavily on the element of surprise.) Nail the gas pedal and as soon as the rope snaps tight, the unit should be picked cleanly off the roof.

Step Two: You have to change the shape of the antenna for our purposes. Be careful. You don't want to alter the reception capabilities of the frequency-tuned components. Hold the antenna like a battering ram and run it into the inside corner of your garage as shown in Diagram B:

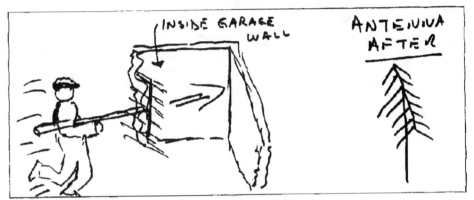

Diagram B

Ram it as many times as necessary until it looks like the picture.

Step Three: You need a front door with the doorknob right in the middle. These doors were extremely popular for about nine days in the early sixties and you'll need to find a house built during that time to find this type of door. The easiest way is to tell a real estate agent that you're looking to buy a house with the front doorknob in the middle of the door. When he takes you through it, look for a calendar in the home that has the vacation trip to Opryland marked, so you'll know when to drop around to get the door. Once you get it, install the front door in your house. Then remove it and take out the doorknob, leaving a hole in the centre of the door.

Step Four: This next step is a little dangerous because you have to drive on the highway. At night. Without your headlights on. Don't come back until you have two of those triangular YIELD signs. Take an adjustable wrench with you. And have a really interesting story to tell the highway patrol, just in case.

Step Five: Using the Handyman's Secret Weapon—duct tape, attach the Yield signs to the door as shown in Diagram C.

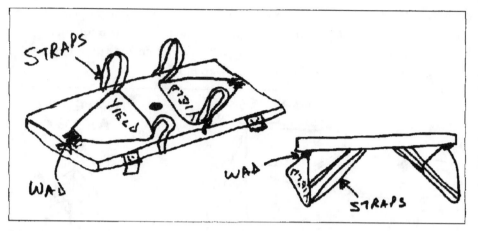

Diagram C

The wad of duct tape at the point works as a hinge. The strips of tape to the corners prevent the signs from swinging out too far. Once they're attached, flip the door over and let the signs swing into place as shown. The door is now a patio table.

Step Six: Remove the pair of awnings from the windows. You can use a screwdriver or the adjustable wrench, or if you're pressed for time, the boat anchor technique is always quick and effective. After removing, duct tape the awnings together and slide them over the bent antenna and down into the doorknob hole as shown in Diagram D.

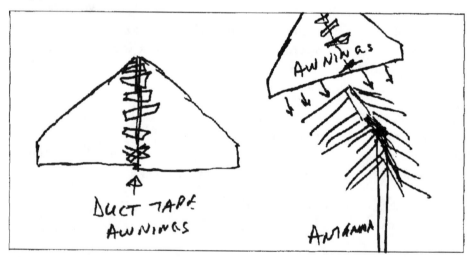

Diagram D

You're now ready to enjoy a full summer of outdoor entertaining. When winter comes, simply reverse the steps and move indoors.

Diagram E

Beautiful Patio Set in Summer

Diagram F

Normal House in Winter

THE GROUND HOG
  By Red Green
It is Spring
The groundhog comes out of his
  hole and sees a shadow
It is the shadow of my right
  front tire
That means Winter will last
  another six weeks
But not for him

If it ain't broke, don't lend it.

UNUSUAL INSECTS OF POSSUM LODGE

ENLARGED
89 X ↙

The Gnurb
Smaller than a gnat. Larger than a midge. 2/3 the size of a fruit fly.
Three times as annoying as any of them.

The Ear Toupee
Very similar to an earwig, but smaller and way more obvious.

The Preaching Mantis
The female devours the male right after they mate and then gets very
self-righteous about it, claiming it's revenge for years of oppression.

The Treb Fly
An imaginary insect for those awkward moments when someone
you're talking to laughs and a hunk of food, or something from their
nose, flies out and sticks to their chin. And rather than say, "Hey,
you've got tuna on your face," or "Better wipe that snot off before the boss sees you," you
can say, "Oops, there's a bug on your face, looks like a little treb fly, better wipe it off."

The Duct Tapeworm
A totally inanimate insect that looks exactly like a discarded strip of duct tape. Usually
found at the sight of Handyman projects that have been completed or abandoned. The
biggest difference between a Duct Tapeworm and a garbage piece of duct tape is that you
can leave the former in its natural habitat whereas the latter has to be rolled into a ball
and put into the trash can, often causing you to miss the first few minutes of "Baywatch."

A POSSUM AS A PET

Naturally everybody wants to have a pet possum, but there are a few things you should
think about before you drive down to the pet store with a handful of money—the first
one being that the pet store doesn't sell them. They may try to sell you something else and
claim it's a possum. Be suspicious, especially if the possum is in an aquarium or has a beak.

What you should buy is a possum trap, which is similar to a raccoon trap except that
when you go to check it, there's a possum inside rather than a raccoon. As you turn your
possum into a pet, there are a few things you should know:

1. Possums are untrainable, disloyal, and pretty stupid.
2. They are not shy about relieving themselves.

But here's the good news—they're edible.

If you're still convinced you want a pet possum, you can look forward to several years
of a one-sided and extremely unfulfilling relationship.

WARNING: Possums have had difficulty surviving in areas with moving vehicles.

WEATHER-WISE

An armchair almanac of woodland wisdom.

Just because you don't have access to a radio, or a television, or a National Weather Service Satellite Computer DownLink doesn't mean you have to be at the mercy of the weather.

The observant outdoorsperson knows that nature signals approaching trouble, giving those who are weather-wise plenty of time to seek shelter where there's a big chair, beverages, chips and a cable TV sports channel.

THUNDERSTORM:	DISTANT: Cicadas stop chirping. Sparrows grow quiet. High thin whispy clouds that look like shredded tube socks. Wolves circle, grow agitated. Ants march in straight lines carrying umbrellas. IMMINENT: Wolves seek shelter under your bed. The guy you're fishing with looks over your shoulder and says, "Uh oh." A loud crack! A flash of light, and you wake up in a hospital.
HAILSTORM:	Ants form into circles. Beavers play poker. Birds visibly agitated and given to unnecessary shoving. Cicadas verbally abusive.
SNOWSTORM:	Dogs nervous and edgy. Squirrels swallow their nuts in fear. Moss seems damp when you stuff it in your pants. Ants start watching NASCAR racing on television.
FLASH FLOOD:	Sparrows stop singing. Ants form into rowing teams. Skunks seen wearing life jackets.
PARTLY CLOUDY, MODERATE TEMPERATURES, CLEARING IN THE THE AFTERNOON:	Sparrows stop singing, start rapping. Beavers nervously twiddle their lips. Chickens lay black eggs.
TORNADOS:	DISTANT: Ants do the hokey pokey. Cicadas burrow into large hairdos. Dogs visibly agitated; cats visibly relaxed. Sheep and goats seek shelter in your basement. IMMINENT: Low black clouds, high white clouds, and a flying shrub. Cows and horses dig bomb shelters.
SUNNY AND CLEAR:	Birds fly in circles. Foxes put on suntan lotion. Fish swim upside down. Trees point upwards.

MEET YOUR MEMBER.

MEET YOUR ASSOCIATE MEMBER

Okay, time now to meet the man who is one of my personal favourites—myself. Okay I said "man" and maybe that's looking into the future but I like doing that 'cause that's where things are going to happen, and it's a lot nicer than looking into the past, especially if you include that high school dance where I was forced to take my sister.

FULL NAME *Harold Dortmund Spooner Mepps Green Junior.*

AGE *Eighteen. No, wait, seventeen. No, eighteen. What month is this? Thursday. Then I'm nineteen.*

MAJOR TURN ONS: *Fast women in loose clothing and Nintendo.*

MAJOR TURN OFFS: *People with tans, getting beaten up, insincerity and thermonuclear war*

FAVOURITE COLOUR: *Dark Chocolate Brown.*

FAVOURITE FOOD:
Dark brown chocolate. That was neat. Dark chocolate and brown, neat.

LAST BOOK READ *Gravity's Rainbow by Thomas Pynchon, no, wait, it was the instructions for my digital watch home video game.*

PROUDEST ACCOMPLISHMENT:
Producing Uncle Red's show. No. Figuring out my digital watch home video game.

TEEN TALK

I know a lot of you teens feel you have to rebel and be obnoxious and embarrass your parents at restaurants, but that's just a normal part of growing up and finding your place in the world, especially when your parents throw you out. Whereas getting a tattoo is stupid. I don't mean those rub-on dealies in the box of Crunchie Critters, I'm talking about a carnival-booth, skin-carved, sober-up-and-scream-about-it tattoo.

A tattoo is basically a liquid sliver. And the liquid is permanent ink. Getting a tattoo is like sucking on a pen with your whole body.

And it's painful. There are only two things more painful than getting a tattoo, the first one being getting two tattoos and the second being getting either of them removed. Maybe there's some appeal in having Guns 'N Roses tattooed on your butt, but sixty years from now, in the middle of your hemorrhoid operation, you're gonna find out why it's not a good idea to get your surgeon laughing.

Wanted, any and all Kathy Lee Gifford record albums. We will pay cash for your Kathy Lee Gifford records. Including her Best of album... and "Kathy Lee Sings Your Favourite Christmas Carols." Contact the Possum Lake Skeet Shooting Club.

"Lost, expensive leather bomber jacket, classic design, rich brown tones, genuine silk lining. Contact Junior Singleton"

"Found, dirty brown vinyl jacket with flimsy nylon lining. Contact Bill."
Junior, good news, talk to Bill.

You can't make a silk purse out of a sow's ear without severely damaging its hearing.

WEEKEND CAMPING HINTS

Step 1. Go on Tuesday. Avoid the crowds.

Step 2. You'll need a good excuse to get off work or to escape from your loved ones or any other unpleasant responsibilities. A good way to do that is to put your own obituary in the paper. This will stop people from looking for you but it only works once. Unless you're Shirley Maclaine.

SUNDAY	MONDAY	TUESDAY	WEDNESDAY	PH
NAP DAY + FOOTBALL	PACK	CAMPING DAY!	PHONE IN SICK	
PHONE HOME	PHONE IN SICK!	PHONE IN SICK!	PHONE IN SICK!	
	PHO	P I—	P L—	

Step 3. Borrow a tent, bedroll, campstove, hamper, cooler, and a portable TV from a friend you can afford to lose. Heave it all into your vehicle. Back out of your driveway and immediately pull into the passing lane. Press your right foot on the accelerator and your left hand on the horn and maintain that position until you run out of gas or hit something, which will signify that it's time to start camping.

Here's a real nice spot

Step 4. If there are other campers already there, go to the biggest, most tattooed guy and have him throw a beer bottle as far as he can. Make sure you camp beyond that. If you don't feel like pitching your own tent, pretend you're having trouble with it and for sure a passing woman of the nineties will stop and do it for you. Exchanging physical work for minor humiliation is an acceptable trade-off for all Possum Lodge members.

Step 5. Instead of building a campfire, find a tall dry tree and ignite it. This is not only an excellent source of heat and light, it will keep away the bugs and also people who wear a lot of hairspray like television evangelists or professional bowlers. For fun, toast up some marshmallows till they're hot and gooey and then drop 'em on the faces of your sleeping friends. When it's time to put the fire out, beer makes an excellent extinguisher as long as you drink it first.

A tree is just a campfire waiting to happen

Step 6. Unroll your sleeping bag on a soft dry surface, such as someone else's sleeping bag. When the owner comes looking, say his bag was swiped by the tattooed guy who threw the bottle. Once you're snug in your sleeping bag, make the loudest and most offensive body noises that you can. This will send a clear message to the other campers and the animal kingdom that nobody should mess with you, you're too busy messing with yourself.

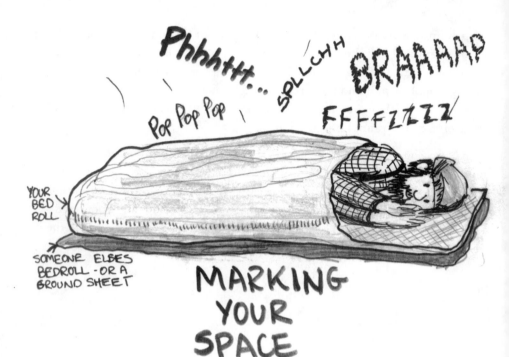

Phhhttt... SPLLCHH BRAAAAP

Pop Pop Pop

FFFFZZZZ

YOUR BED ROLL

SOMEONE ELSES BEDROLL - OR A GROUND SHEET

MARKING YOUR SPACE

Step 7. On the off chance that you live 'til morning, get up quietly and collapse everybody else's tents. This will create a certain amount of confusion and even hostility so none of them will notice you syphoning their gas.

Step 8. Grab an armful of other people's cookware and hit the road. The disappointment of having to return to your job or family will be offset by the fun of whipping pots and pans at hitchhikers.

Step 9. Go back to your normal life and count the days until Tuesday.

```
good with a knife
Trapper Jack was hunting bear
A dangerous hobby at best
They brought him back to the
    doctor in town
And he was a heck of a mess
There was some assembly required
Mostly teeth and bones and hair
Jack had always been good with a knife
But unfortunately not quite as good as the bear
```

Okay, time now to meet the man who disproves the adage about what's in a name. Not a loner by nature, he has had to adapt to the stand-offish attitude of others. A great concept guy, he has always been weak at execution and is not seen as a team player. He may get it together some day, especially if he gets running water.

STINKY PETERSON

FULL NAME: Stephen Riechen Puanteur Peterson

AGE: 35

OCCUPATION: Jack of All Trades.

MARITAL STATUS: Master of none.

HOBBIES: Catching, cleaning and frying up a mess of catfish. Hunting, cleaning and frying up moose. Watching stock car races on TV.

MAJOR TURN ONS: Intelligent, urban, career-oriented women who share my hobbies.

He's on the dock; this is as close as the photographer would get.

MAJOR TURN OFFS: Cleanliness freaks.

FAVOURITE COLOUR: Puce.

FAVOURITE FOOD: Chili, garlic, cabbage, beer, pickled eggs.

FAVOURITE MOVIES: "Gone With The Wind". "The Air Up There". "The Blue Angel".

FAVOURITE BOOKS: "The Fisherman's Bible". "The Hunter's Bible". "TV Guide".

PROUDEST ACCOMPLISHMENT: I haven't done it yet, but when I do, you'll be the first to know. After Claudia Schiffer of course.

LODGE RESPONSIBILITIES: Organizing hunting, fishing and TV events.

BUDDY SYSTEM

Okay, you're pulling in the driveway. It's late and you didn't say you were gonna be late and you know you're not gonna be able to sneak into the house and you know the first thing you're gonna hear. "Why didn't you call?!" And you're gonna need an answer, and you're gonna need truth, and the truth is you don't have an answer.

So the truth is, you have to make one up. And it's gonna have to be a hummer, eh? So I'm gonna make some up for you now, and then you can use 'em when the time comes. You might say, "I gave all my money to a homeless family who were living in the parking lot garbage bin and I didn't have the heart to ask for change so I could use the phone."

Or you could try this... "The police are tracking a reported invasion of aliens who are pure energy and they asked everybody at the bar, including the table dancers, not to use the phone."

Or you could say "I'm real sorry that I didn't call. It was thoughtless. Please forgive me. I love you very much." But try the other two first.

```
SPRING RISE
  By Red Green
It is Spring
Your kite soars
  into the sky
Rising on the
  thermals
The string
  shorts out the
  power lines
You rise in your
  thermals
```

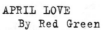

```
APRIL LOVE
  By Red Green
On a sunny April day years ago my
  mother turned sweet sixteen.
And my father met my mother on another sunny April day
And on a third sunny day in April, they first kissed and
  fell in love.
And another April day they wed as the sun shone from above.
And I was born yet another sunny day in April.
I'm told that was one of the few years we had five sunny
  days in a row.
```

RED GREEN—
THE TELEVISION YEARS

Actually "The Red Green Show" is not my first stab at television. That surprises most people who've seen it. Over the years I've hosted a large number of outdoors shows and nature films. Here's some of my other work which you may or may not have seen and/or enjoyed. I have everything I've ever done recorded on tape. (Mostly BETA and some 8 tracks.)

"The Lure of Lures" (1971-74) Lure-Id Films Inc. 26 episodes. Every week I talked for a half hour about fishing lures. My guests included Old Man Sedgwick, Junior Singleton and a very young Michelle Pfeiffer. This series can sometimes be seen in reruns after 4 a.m. on small cable channels during thunderstorms.

Mr. Bait Commercials (1975-77) I was the official spokesperson for the Mr. Bait Shop in town. I loaned my face and my good name to promote their fine line of fishing bait. Most people don't remember seeing me in those commercials—perhaps because my face was somewhat obscured by the giant worm costume.

Run Kids! It's A Big Bad Fire! (1978) This was a film I made for the local fire department. It was an educational film to warn school children about the danger of playing with matches. To save money we filmed it at my house. Ironically one of the bright movie lights set fire to a stack of empties and burned the place

down. The profits from the film almost covered the $500.00 deductible on my fire insurance policy.

"Let's Fry Something Good" (1980-3) Fry Films Inc. 45 episodes. This was a cooking show I did with my wife Bernice. Each week she would fry up a different meal—fish, chicken, spaghetti. I would sit on a stool and banter with her and ask questions like, "Is that a real apple?" Then at the end of the show I would taste what Bernice had prepared

and smile at the camera and go "MMmmmmmMMM!" (Golly, that was acting.) Series was cancelled when my cholesterol level surpassed our ratings.

"Understanding Computers" (1984) An educational TV series about understanding and using your brand new home computer. I hosted the show and played the part of the viewer—the person who knows nothing about computers. Over the series I learned all about software and hardware and so on from my tutor—played by my then 5-year-old nephew, Harold. The show had a good budget, a great time slot, and lots of snazzy special effects. Our only mistake was choosing the Mattel Intellivision as our computer.

"Cars and Bikinis" (1985) Headlight Productions. Pilot episode only. This was a great idea that never went to series. Kinda like "Baywatch," but with cars too. Just too ahead of its time.

"Explosions!" (1986) BoomBoom Films. Pilot episode only. This was an educational series about the history of things exploding and blowing up. An unfortunate incident during filming shut the project down. Later the A&E network bought the idea off me for $30.00 and retitled it "Brute Force," and it was a hit. Timing is everything. As we learned during that unfortunate incident during filming.

"Buster and the Fat Man" (1987-8) Thriller Productions. (4 Made for Canadian

Cable TV Mystery Movies of the Week.) I moved behind the camera to try my hand at writing, directing, producing, set designing, costume designing, lighting, gripping, publicizing and editing. Concept: Moose Thompson and Buster Hadfield starred as a couple of wisecracking detectives who walk a fine line between danger and comedy and justice. Moose plays The Fat Man, an ex-cop and circus sword swallower. Buster Hadfield played Buster Fadhield, a former con, born in England, raised by wolves, and now rebuilding his life. We re-used a lot of footage from "Explosions!" and "Cars & Bikinis." It was a great concept, lots of fun, but making the two lead characters Siamese twins was, in hindsight, a mistake. The titles of the four movies are "Dial 911 For Murder," "Love & Larceny & Larry," "The Maltese Possum" and "Murder Most Lousy." These movies can still be seen in reruns at my house when there's nothing else on and I'm feeling sorry for myself.

Acid Rain!! What Acid Rain? (1988) Produced by the Association of Canadian Mining Corporations. 22 minutes. Another educational film I made on behalf of a bunch of very big companies. During filming I learned a whole bunch of stuff about the environment I didn't know before. The upbeat message of this film is that Mother Nature is a lot more resilient than we think.

"The Red Green Show" (1990) followed by **"The New Red Green Show."** (1994) Twenty years of television experience collided with my nephew Harold, and the rest, as they say, is history...

HAROLD SPEAKS.

Okay. Being a Teenager. Okay. It's not easy being a teenager. And I'm not just talking about pimples and braces and hormones and rejection and fear and career worries and school marks and no friends and failing driving school and peer pressure and stubbing your toe a lot. I'm talking about being almost an adult.

When you're eighteen you can fight for your country, well not really, we don't have a war, and we don't have an army really, but we might.

The point is, your parents run your life. Why can't we be trusted to be, like, responsible for our own lives and for taking care of ourselves? Why can't our parents butt out of our lives and worry about their own responsibilities such as cleaning our rooms and giving us allowance and making our meals and driving us everywhere and buying us computers and stuff? They can't do all those things if they're busy telling us to be home at a certain time or get better grades or chew with our mouths full. Thank you.

```
THE TOBOGGAN
   By Red Green
It is Winter
Time to get your
   old sled out
And swoosh down
   giant hills
To learn to hang
   on tight
And have those high
   speed thrills

The good old sled
   will show you
How to fly and soar
   and whiz
And teach you just
   how hard
A frozen elm tree
   really is
```

```
HIP WADERS
   By Red Green
It is Spring
Trout season
You wade into the
   stream waist-high
You feel water run
   down your legs
There's a hole
   in your hip waders
You hope.
```

Honk if you hate noise pollution.

CHEAP & CHIC!

**Three Charming Decorator Accents Made From Stuff
You'd Normally Throw Out**

BOWLING BALL FLOWER POT

Got an old bowling ball that's dented or broken or always
flies into the gutter for some reason? Don't toss it! Turn it into
a lovely ebony flower holder.

> HOW? Clamp the ball in a large vice, so the finger-holes
> face down. Sand the top side of the ball
> somewhat flat. Remove from vice. Turn the ball
> over so it rests on its flat surface. Put flowers in the finger holes.
> (Drill more holes for a fuller bouquet.)

BABY'S PLAYPEN WINE RACK

Have your babies grown up and reached drinking age? Don't throw out their old
playpen. Because your kids'll probably get married, have nine kids, lose their job,
and announce they're moving back into your home.

If you get lucky and they don't move back, why not turn that
playpen into a lovely wine rack? After all with the kids gone,
now you can afford some nice wine.

> HOW? Disassemble the playpen, making sure not to
> wreck the four sides. Take two sides and lay one
> on top of the other, at right angles, so that the posts
> form a cross pattern. Screw, nail, glue, or—better still—duct tape
> the two sides together. Repeat with the remaining two sides. Join them
> with short lengths of wood. And you've got a wine rack! Now fill it
> with baby bottles of homemade beer. Then when you're thirsty, grab a
> bottle and suck on the nipple. Is that heaven or what?

STEAM RAD CIRCUS CALLIOPE!

When you convert your house from hot-water radiator heating to forced-air gas,
save a couple of those old iron radiators. They'll make a great steam calliope, just
like the old circuses used to have before they all went bankrupt.

> HOW? I'm not sure. Our house has electric
> baseboard heaters. But it shouldn't be hard.

I wanna talk to all you middle-aged guys about fading urges, the sense that you are maybe not the passionate lover you once were, at least the way you tell it.

Okay, first of all, the fact that you've changed from a young stag who is eager to rut into an old drag who's stuck in a rut is a good thing. 'Cause there is less chance you'll become a father at a time when you no longer have, say, the patience or the energy or the brain-power to help with homework.

Another upside to the loss of your sex drive is that this means once or twice a week, for a few fleeting minutes, you'll actually be able to concentrate on other stuff, like say your job. A lot of the great discoveries have been made by old guys. Colonel Saunders was almost retired before he got the inspiration to dedicate his life to fried chicken. Or how about the famous 70-year-old television producer Aaron Spelling? Nobody who's still sexually active could come up with a concept like "The Love Boat."

So I say just accept the declining desire. Your wife is probably just as happy to read in bed and you get to watch all the hockey games, even if there's overtime. Remember, I'm pulling for ya 'cause we're all in this together.

```
DISAPPOINTMENT
   By Red Green
It is winter.
The lake freezes
   flat as a table.
With delight you
   discover
   it supports your
   weight.
With disappointment
   you discover it won'
   support the weight
   of your snowmobile.
Oh boy.
```

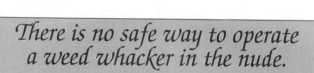

There is no safe way to operate a weed whacker in the nude.

Okay, time now to meet the man who was around when country wasn't cool. Seen by some as a living tourist attraction, he's viewed by many as an eyesore, requiring more maintenance than he's worth. A lifelong collector of historical Possum Lake trivia, he's already forgotten more than he'll ever know. Everyone knows that he won't be around forever but it'll sure feel like it.

OLD MAN SEDGWICK

Old Man Sedgwick at age 12

FULL NAME: Orville Lloyd Dutton Manly Alvin Norbert Sedgwick. (O.L.D. M.A.N. Sedgwick for short)

AGE: Pre-cambrian.

OCCUPATION: Retired. Can't remember what I did before that.

MARITAL STATUS: Widowed. Several times I think.

HOBBIES: Playing with my teeth. Complaining.

MAJOR TURN ONS: Waking up, and going to the bathroom.

MAJOR TURN OFFS: Going to the bathroom, and then waking up.

FAVOURITE COLOUR: Gray.

FAVOURITE FOOD: Mushy stuff.

FAVOURITE MOVIES: Anything with the Gish sisters. Ooh la la!

FAVOURITE BOOKS: I liked "David Copperfield" when it first came out.

PROUDEST ACCOMPLISHMENT: Outliving all my stinking family members.

LODGE RESPONSIBILITIES: I am the lodge's living history record. Members often ask me about ancient traditions, past events and where dangerous stuff was buried so we don't dig it up by accident.

WORD SEARCH

Here's a Word Search Puzzle for those quiet evenings when there's nothing on TV because all the professional athletes have gone on strike again.

The Theme of this Word Search is "Kinds of Fish!"

_____WORD LIST_____

LAKETROUT	CATFISH	ROOK
ROCK BASS	SUNFISH	PERCH
COD	HAMMERHEAD	WALLEYE
STURGEON	PICKEREL	TUNA
LARGEMOUTH	PIKE	MUSKIE
MINNOW	SMALLMOUTH	EELS
SHARKS	GOLDFISH	SALMON
MINNOWS	GROUPER	TURBOT
BASS	ANGELFISH	KIPPERS

```
L A K E T R O U T C A T F I S H R O O K

R O C K B A S S S U N F I S H P E R C H

C O D H A M M E R H E A D W A L L E Y E

S T U R G E O N P I C K E R E L T U N A

L A R G E M O U T H P I K E M U S K I E

M I N N O W S M A L L M O U T H E E L S

S H A R K S G O L D F I S H S A L M O N

M I N N O W S G R O U P E R T U R B O T

B A S S A N G E L F I S H K I P P E R S
```

THE RED GREEN CROSSWORD!

ACROSS

1. The ___ Green Show
2. Harold's Uncle
3. Colour of blood
4. Fire truck colour
5. F___ Flintstone
6. Singer Helen ___dy
7. USA Flag: ___ white & blue
8. Homonym of read
9. Fake clue: ___ herring
10. A business loss: ___ ink
11. Type of star: ___ giant
12. Overnight flight: ___-eye
13. Member of a paramilitary youth organization in China during the Cultural Revolution of the 1960s: ___ Guard
14. Colour of ketchup
15. Hue of Macintosh apple

DOWN

1. Head of Possum Lodge
2. "___ sky at night, sailor's delight."
3. A member of the Congregation of Most Holy Redeemer, in Italy during the 1700s: ___emptorist
4. Played the father on TV show "Sanford & Son": ___d Foxx
5. Colour of ripe tomatoes
6. Shade of crimson
7. Mixed with white to produce pink
8. Heat is infra___ light
9. "Roll out the ___ carpet"
10. Colour of strawberries
12. Colour of raspberries
13. Colour of maraschino cherries
14. "Was my face ___."
15. Communist (slang)

HOW STRONG IS YOUR MARRIAGE?

For all you guys who are married, or just act like you are, here's The Possum Lodge version of the Cosmo Quiz. The questions apply to both men and women. You and your significant other should answer these questions honestly and openly. Just never ever show each other your answers.

1. My marriage is more important to me than:

     A) my work.

     B) my weekend.

     C) my own chances for long term happiness.

2. When I have a serious problem I know I can count on my spouse to:

     A) be there for me.

     B) laugh at me.

     C) be the source of it all.

     D) blab it to all his/her friends.

3. My spouse and I laugh at the same things:

     A) usually.

     B) seldom.

     C) only if they happen to me.

4. I would say that my spouse feels our sex life is:

     A) exciting.

     B) adequate.

     C) distracting.

     D) a vague memory.

5. I think it's important for a couple to share the same...

     A) values.

     B) religious beliefs.

     C) cutlery.

     D) undershorts.

6. My spouse bought special fancy silk undergarments for me to wear...

    A) now and then.

    B) all the time.

    C) when my hernia flares up.

7. On our honeymoon my spouse and I discovered...

    A) how much we loved each other.

    B) how much we loved hot tubs.

    C) how much we loved all the great movies on the hotel's Pay-TV.

8. As a couple we try to set aside quality time for each other...

    A) at least twice a day.

    B) at least once a week.

    C) during commercials.

9. Which famous couple are you most like?

    A) Romeo and Juliet.

    B) Edith and Archie.

    C) Sonny and Cher.

    D) The *Bismarck* and the *Hood*.

10. If my spouse and I had to do it all over again, knowing what we know now...

    A) we would get married again.

    B) we would live together first.

    C) I'd kill myself.

    D) I'd kill him/her.

    E) I'd hold out for a bigger dowry.

    F) I'd hold out for a bigger everything.

    G) I'd hold out.

CONNECT THE DOTS

Parents: Here's a puzzle that'll keep your kids busy for a whole summer!

Hey Kids! What is it?

Connect the Dots & See!

Connect EVERY dot with EVERY other dot!   Don't peek at the answer!

What is it? Answer: A Black Hole in Space!

LEARN TO DRAW THE RED GREEN WAY!

Anyone who can put a pencil to paper can learn to draw!
I guarantee it*

To paint a floor or a wall, you just start in one corner and paint until you reach the opposite corner. (Hopefully one with a door or you're trapped.)

To paint a picture, an artist doesn't just start in one corner of the canvas and paint until he or she reaches the opposite corner. It's true!

Artists build up their picture slowly, adding elements to the composition to gradually create the final effect.

And if it's good enough for the artists, it's good enough for us, right?

TALK IS CHEAP, LET'S DRAW!

Here's my step-by-step method. From circle to a self-portrait in 6 steps!

1	2	3
Draw shape of head.	Sketch in eyes, ears, & nose.	Add mouth, & details.

4	5	6
Hair, beard, other details.	Preliminary shading.	Harold, paste a photo of me here before you send this off to the publisher. Do final shading, and Voila!

PRETEND YOU'RE TED TURNER AND COLOURIZE "AN ADVENTURE WITH BILL"

I find Bill in his kayak.

I help him into the water.

Bill wedges his butt into the kayak.

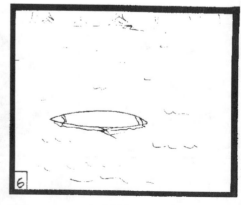

I remove it non-surgically.

Bill goes out in his kayak.

Bill goes over in his kayak.

Bill waves.

I wave back.

Bill waves harder.

I wave back.

Bill is getting way out there.

I realize he's not waving.

I go fast in my boat.

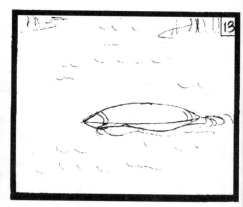

Bill moves closer.

Too much closer. Bang!

Bill moves away again.

Bill goes into permanent dry dock.

He who laughs last, just got it.

BUDDY SYSTEM

Okay, there are certain things that the woman in your life may ask you and you won't have time to think about your answer. The worst one being, "Am I fat?" Now for sure you're not gonna say "yes" unless you have a death wish, but you even gotta say "No" the right way or this conversation'll be going into triple overtime. Just say "No." Right away. As soon as she asks. Just say "No." Just like that. No pause. No thinkin' it over. No sayin' "Well... no, not really."

But you can't go too far the other way either. You can't say, "What you? Fat? Ha! Get serious. Don't make me laugh! Tell me another one, eh! Sure, all your friends are fat, and so are your sisters, but not you! No way! You're like an underfed chicken. It's sickening how thin you are." 'Cause as Shakespeare said eh, "Methinks the lady doth process too much."

"Attention fellow Possums. I, Moose Thompson, have figured out how to get my VCR to stop flashing 12, 12, 12. Just unplug it when you're not using it."

So when she asks "Am I fat?" just say "No," and then ask her to go out for dinner. That way you'll look like a hero and, since she's worried about her weight, she'll probably refuse the invitation. It's a win, win.

If a tree falls in the woods and nobody hears the lumberjack yell "Timber" does the guy it lands on make a sound?

HAROLD SPEAKS.

Okay. Getting a bad report card. Okay first question. How bad? Failing? Having to repeat a year? Or having to go back to kindergarten and start over. That's very time-consuming.

Okay supposing your parents are not pleased, let's say. And kids tease you and throw your lunch into the girls' showers. It happens. Just tell them that academic achievement is a trivial and inconsequential piece of flocking in the rich tapestry of life.

And also point out that Einstein did bad in school. Or is it badly? Thank you.

ON A STARRY NIGHT
  By Red Green
It is winter.
They say on a cold
  clear winter night.
If you go outside and
  look up.
You'll see a hundred
  stars shining
  overhead.
But if you stand
  there long enough
The dark works its
  magic
And soon you'll see a
  thousand stars
And then ten thousand
  twinkling specks.
And eventually the
  cold will freeze
  your head into a
  block of ice
And when you fall
  backwards on the
  hard ground
Your frozen brain
  will shatter into a
  million pieces.
So I'm staying inside
  and watching reruns
  of "The A-Team."

horse racing
I'd rather have been born a racehorse
That sounds like a pretty good go
With a trainer and a ninety-pound jockey
Who'd ride me for a minute or so
I'd win the daily double
The Trifecta and the Exactor
Cause I know what a stud farm is
And motivation would be a significant factor

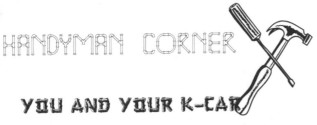

YOU AND YOUR K-CAR

At one time or another most of us have owned a K-Car. Perhaps it was a gift or a "real steal of a deal" or maybe someone just dumped one into the ravine out back of your house. Eventually all of us K-Car owners come the conclusion that our K-Car is no longer living up to the second syllable of its name. But just because it's no longer a good car doesn't mean you should have it scrapped or sell it to a relative whose safety you don't care much about.

Instead let that K-Car be the basis of an exciting handyman project. Turn that defect into an asset!

Here are some ideas to get you thinking. Remember, imagination costs nothing.

1. The "Car"-den Shed

The water pump is connected to a hose for watering the lawn. Tools are stored in the trunk. The tires have been cut in half and used to line the driveway. Headlights are garden nightlights.

2. The "K"-bin Cruiser

Wheels removed and wheel wells duct-taped over to provide a seamless hull. Engine mounted on back trunk as an outboard. Tires used as bumpers along side of boat. Back seat mounted on roof, with windshield in front and steering wheel, to be a flying bridge. Two front seats mounted on the back as fishing seats. Fishing rod made from antennas. Radio tuned to marine bands.

3. The Ja-"K"-uzzi!

The roof is cut off, the interior is lined with a swimming pool liner and the water pump runs in and circulates water through the heater to heat it and then into the jacuzzi. The radio is mounted on the trunk lid.

4. Mon-"K"-Bars:

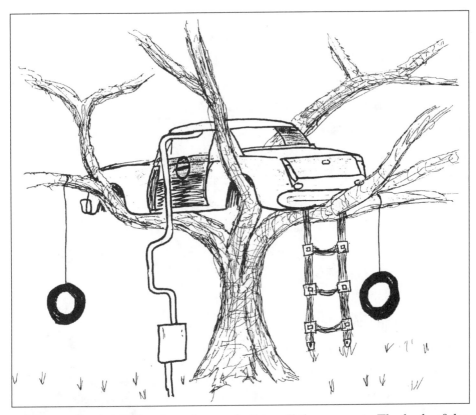

A swing set/gym/climber/tree fort made from all the car parts. The body of the car is up a tree. The muffler and tailpipe make a pole to slide down. The two seats are mounted on a board for a teeter-totter. The tires are swings. The back seat is a loveseat/swing. The engine and drive train are hooked up to spin the hood like a merry-go-round. Door handles provide handles for kids to hang on.

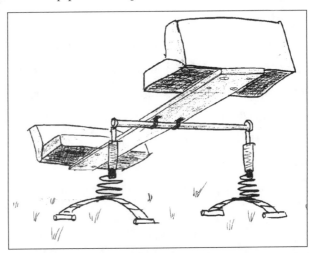

NORTH OF 40

I wanna talk to you middle-aged guys about job security. I've had a few jobs myself over the years so I know the pink slip warning signs. Like if you skip off work for a day and nobody notices, that's a bad sign. Or your boss keeps showing new employees around your office and asking them, "What about here?" That's not good. Or you take a one week holiday and they replace you with a twelve-year-old kid who doesn't speak English. Then when you return he gets a going-away party where everybody cries. And your boss writes down the kid's home number. Bad signs.

So if this sounds familiar to you, there are several steps you can take to prepare for the inevitable disaster.

Step one: marry someone who has a job. Step two: get on a first name basis with everybody at the unemployment insurance place. But most of all don't get down on yourself. Try to look on the bright side of being unemployed. Your time's your own. No traffic problems—you wake up in the morning; you're there.

When I was between jobs, from early June of 1982 to late August... of '89, I managed to keep my head up. A lot of people are working hard making money doing something they don't enjoy—work; whereas you're taking it easy making zip doing something you love—nothin'. It's not such a bad trade-off. Remember, I'm pulling for ya 'cause we're all in this together.

THE WHIPPOORWILL
By Red Green
It is Spring
The whippoorwill
calls out in the
early dawn
"You missed me.
You missed me."
Everyone reloads.

BUYING TIP$

TIP$ ON INVESTMENTS

Thinking of investing in the stock market? Or mutual funds?
Or land in Florida? Here are some things to look for,
and some things to watch out for in any investment opportunity.

GOOD IGN

+ Your investment is insured.

+ Investment company has their own letterhead, not stationery from a local motel.

+ Other investors include large companies, well-known business figures or members of organized crime.

+ The mutual fund never invests in Canadian-made movies or sit-coms.

+ Bill & Hillary invested in it.

BAD IGN

− Salesman only lets you read every other page of the documents you have to sign.

− Salesman wears a paper bag on his head.

− Fine print on contract is in a foreign language.

− Your dividends will be paid in Monopoly money.

− Your investment counsellor drives a pink Cadillac with huge fuzzy dice, fun fur interior and the licence plate is "TUFF GUY."

− Head of investment fund has to borrow cab fare to get home.

− They promise a million percent annual profit on your investment.

− To receive your share of the profits, your wife has to do something that was in the movie *Indecent Proposal*.

− To receive your share of the profits, you have to do something from the movie *The Godfather*.

OTHER BOOKS
FROM POSSUM LODGE

The Red Green Book isn't the first book to come out of Possum Lodge. Although it may be the first to go in.

Here are other books we have put out over the years, with their authors, date of publication, and a brief synopsis of what the book's about.

All of them were self-published on our old Gestetner machine so copies may be difficult to obtain. No library would touch 'em. And I doubt if even the guys who wrote them kept a copy.

MORE THAN ONE WAY TO SKIN A CAT *by Young Man Sedgwick. (published 1947)* A quick guide to home taxidermy. Earn big bucks and huge dough by gutting and stuffing big bucks and huge does.

LET'S GO HUNTING! *by Morris Bern (Oct 1947)* Hunting is easy, just grab a gun, and go!

LET'S LEARN HOW TO TREAT A GUNSHOT WOUND! *by Morris Bern (Nov. 1947)* The human body is a very complicated thing to fix.

ODE TO A STUMP *by Orville Torpid (1951)* A collection of poems about nature from a guy who didn't get out much.

ODE TO A LOG *by Orville Torpid (1952)* Another collection of poems from a guy who obviously hasn't found happiness.

ODE TO A TOAD *by Orville Torpid (1953)* The final collected works of a poet who probably died a virgin.

115 CRAFT PROJECTS FROM PINECONES *by Herbert Balderson (1959)* Includes projects like making a pinecone back-scratcher, a roto-rooter and an entire set of living room furniture.

DO DEW WORMS SCREAM ON MY HOOK? *by Wally Pendrake. (1963)* Philosophical musings on fishing by a fellow who was out in the sun for way too long.

MY CORVAIR IS PERFECTLY SAFE *by Jasper Spooley. (1965)* Jasper bought a Corvair and spent the rest of his life trying to prove it wasn't a mistake.

A MESS OF BASS, A JUG OF BOOZE AND THOU *by Norbert Puckley. (1967)* Collection of love poems. Best of the bunch, "Love Handles."

HOW TO REVIVE A MARRIAGE *by Larry Dortmund. (1971)* One man's sensitive, soul-searching quest to get his wife's permission to sleep around a lot.

THE HISTORY OF CASTRATION *by Mary Dortmund. (1971)* A pretty blunt rebuttal to the previous volume.

2000 COMPLETELY ORIGINAL JOKES *by Buster Hadfield. (1977)* Buster was the comedian in his family. So he collected everything that got a laugh at family gatherings. Sample joke: Q: What's brown, has four doors, and no tires. A: Uncle Gary's new car. (Very funny if you were a Hadfield and you were drunk at a family gathering.)

THE KAMA-KAZIE SUTRA *by "M." (1978)* Unusual love-making positions that can kill you.

WHAT'S WRONG WITH EVERYONE EXCEPT ME? *by Old Man Sedgwick. (1979)* 88 pages of rambling vitriol about everything from the metric system to bell bottom pants to free love to the AMC Pacer. Andy Rooney Eat Your Heart Out. (Actually, that was the title of the first chapter.)

THE CONDENSED BIBLE *by Junior Singleton (1981)* An interesting and scholarly revision of an earlier work. Junior shows how the 7th Commandment was actually Thou Shalt Commit Adultery. All profits from this book went to his ex-wife.

CB RADIO, THE WAVE OF THE FUTURE *by Dougie Franklin. (1981)* With the surge of interest in CB radio, the growing number of CB songs and movies, Dougie shows that by the year 1997 everyone in the world will have their own CB radio, and face-to-face communication will be obsolete.

GOLF MY WAY *by Bob Stuyvesant. (1986)* A How-Not-To Book

THE LONELINESS OF THE LONG-DISTANCE STANDER *by Ranger Gord (1991)* Thinly veiled autobiography. Whatever you do, don't read Chapter 9, about his sex life.

Never underestimate how far you can throw a baked potato.

THE LAST WORD

I thought I'd end this book with one last word to all you middle-aged guys out there who, for one reason or another, have abandoned your dreams. Maybe you dreamed of being an astronaut and ended up as a space cadet. Maybe you dreamed of being an award-winning statesman and ended up a ward of the state. Maybe you dreamed of being an Amway salesman and you are.

Whatever the disappointment, at this time in our lives we shouldn't be bitter. Maybe we set our goals too high. Personally, I wanted to set the world land speed record in a rocket car that I designed, engineered, and built. But, in retrospect, my dream was a bit of a longshot. Especially after I dropped out of junior high.

As we head into the last half of our lives we should still be ambitious, but we need more realistic dreams. Like vowing to go to your grave with at least one of your own teeth. Or doing something nice for someone every day, even if it's to not tell them what you're thinking. I'll follow my dreams no matter how old or worn out I get. Even if I end up in a wheelchair. In fact I'm designing one with a rocket engine. Remember, I'm pulling for ya 'cause we're all in this together.

If you can't stay young,
you can at least stay immature.

EPILOGUE

Coming soon: The SECOND Red Green Book in a row

HERE ARE SOME OF THE MANY INTERESTING AND
ENTERTAINING THINGS YOU'LL FIND IN THE NEXT
RED GREEN BOOK*.

- The Intricacies of Hang Gliding and How to Make a Leg Splint
- The Importance of Intimidation When Running a Service Business
- Friendly Ways of Keeping the Neighbours the Hell Off Your Property
- Avoiding Activity as a Lifestyle
- The Importance of Excess Gas in the Need to Find Your own Space
- The Exciting New Technologies That Are Coming Soon, and How to Sound Like You Understand Them
- The Importance of Pretending You're Interested in other People
- How to Get Your Wife and Kids to Do What You Want So You can Have More Family Time Together
- How to Cook a Three-Course Meal and How to Scrape It Off the Ceiling
- Red Reviews the Toshiba 486DX Laptop with Active Matrix Monitor and Built-in Fax/Modem
- How to Turn Your Van into a Bed and Breakfast

* Assuming the publisher is willing to do this again